Sex and Gender

Student Projects and Exercises

Cheryl A. Rickabaugh

University of Redlands

Boston, Massachusetts   Burr Ridge, Illinois   Dubuque, Iowa
Madison, Wisconsin   New York, New York   San Francisco, California   St. Louis, Missouri

McGraw-Hill

A Division of The **McGraw·Hill** *Companies*

Sex and Gender: Student Projects and Exercises

1 2 3 4 5 6 7 8 9 0 BKM/BKM 9 0 9 8 7

ISBN 0-07-052618-4

www.mhhe.com

CONTENTS

iii

5. GENDER IDENTITY DEVELOPMENT

6. COGNITION, EDUCATION, AND ACHIEVEMENT

7. GENDER AND THE WORKPLACE

8. SEXUALITY

PREFACE

Sex and Gender: Student Projects and Exercises is a workbook designed to supplement an introductory text in sex and gender. The twelve chapters reflect the topical organization of most texts and are representative of most areas of research in the field. Each chapter consists of activities that require students to engage in critical thinking about theoretical constructs and issues, as well as empirical research. An important focus of this workbook is the manner in which race, ethnicity, social class, and sexual orientation interact in the social construction of gender.

Many projects require students to conduct observations, collect data, and review their results within the context of research and theory. In some cases, students replicate classic experiments in the field and critically evaluate their results. Experiential and autobiographical exercises that involve self-reflection and application of the course material to students' experiences also are included. In every instance, students are encouraged to engage in active learning about sex and gender.

I would like to thank a number of people who assisted me on this project. The staff at the University of Redlands Armacost Library, especially Sandi Richey, worked diligently to help me research sources, obtain copyright information, and simply attend to details. A special thanks is due to Beth Kaufman, "Editor Extraordinaire", who planted the seeds of the project and, with the help of her staff at McGraw-Hill, provided assistance and support during all phases of the project. The following reviewers provided helpful comments, suggestions, and guidance along the way: Patricia L. N. Donat, Mississippi University for Women; Angela R. Gillem, Beaver College; C. Lee Harrington, Miami University (Ohio); Hannah Lerman, private practice; Cynthia L. Miller, State University of New York at Oneonta; Julie K. Noram, Wellesley College; Cynthia Poe, Belleville Area College; Cheryl Rappsilber, Amarillo College; Candace Rypisi, Colorado State University; Geraldine Butts Stahly, California State University-San Bernardino; and Sandra S. Tangri, Howard University.

Cheryl A. Rickabaugh

TO THE INSTRUCTOR

This student workbook has been designed to be used as a supplement to college texts in the areas of sex and gender, gender-role development and socialization, and the psychology of women and men. These exercises and activities have been designed with two purposes in mind. First, you may use the projects to form the foundation for in-class discussion of topics introduced in the text and lecture. Students might complete an entire activity in the classroom or prepare materials before class. In either case, students would be engaged in active learning and critical thinking as they apply the concepts from the course to a specific learning situation. You also may use this workbook as a pool of homework assignments that could supplement exam grades and be incorporated into the grading criteria for the course.

I encourage you to customize this workbook to meet your course objectives and to reflect its focus. This book contains too many exercises to be used in a semester, so select the exercises that best meet your needs and illustrate the topics addressed in your course. I hope that the following suggestions will help you to integrate these exercises in your syllabus and use them in your classroom:

1. The projects involving data collection may be adapted in a number of ways. As they are written, each student collects data and summarizes the results in a short written form. A number of variations could be used to meet the goals and structure of your course, including the following:

    *   If your course has an emphasis on research methodology and data analysis, have students collect and submit raw data. The aggregated data set could be analyzed by you or the class. With each student collecting data from one or more participants, a relatively large sample can be easily obtained.

    *   Have students collect their data individually and complete exercises in small groups. Students can compare their data with other members of their group (and, ideally, see that not everyone's data look like theirs). Small groups then collaborate on the summary questions and report their results to the class. This adaptation reduces the amount of time students spend on outside work and encourages cooperative learning.

    *   Materials can be brought to class (by you, your teaching assistant, or students) and the exercises can be completed by small groups. Activities involving content analyses (e.g., Project 1.1) or evaluation of written material (e.g., Project 2.5) are well suited to small group work. Other projects (e.g., Project 2.1 or Project 4.4) can be completed individually or in small groups. Small groups also are useful in brainstorming and preparing students for conducting their own work

outside of class. These groups could identify operational definitions of variables used in analyses (e.g., Project 5.3) or generate ideas for individual activities (e.g., Project 1.4).

- Another useful adaptation is helpful for instructors whose courses have a developmental approach or consider group differences. Encourage your class to increase the heterogeneity of respondents by assigning students to recruit participants from different groups. For example, ask students to collect data from respondents from specific age categories and compare results as a function of age.

- Caution students about the tentativeness of any conclusions that they draw based upon a limited sample of respondents. Do encourage them to compare and contrast their findings with the primary text and class lecture and discussion. References to the research and theory on which these exercises are based are included to assist you in lecture and discussion preparation.

2. Each exercise can be used to support short writing assignments that develop critical thinking skills. A portfolio of written work could be used in lieu of a longer term paper (a description of this method can be found in the paper referenced below). For example, have students complete the autobiographical assignments (e.g., Project 3.3 or Project 6.2) as individual "free writes" in class. After completing the exercise in class, assign a formal essay that requires students to reflect upon the in-class discussion.

3. Encourage students to go beyond their experience and consider a diversity of experiences and expressions. Most data sheets include a space to make note of demographic variables such as occupation, social class, sexual orientation, race/ethnicity, etc. Ask students not to rely upon family members and friends and seek out participants that differ on these variables. Emphasize the comparison of diverse experiences to the results of research, much of which is based upon homogeneous samples.

4. Last, but not least, remind students to read and follow the guidelines given in the "To the Student" section that follows. This section outlines some basic issues of research sampling, the ethical treatment of participants, and how to use this workbook to critically reflect upon the course material.

Reference: Rickabaugh, C. A. (1993). The psychology portfolio: Promoting writing and critical thinking about psychology. *Teaching of Psychology, 20,* 170–172.

TO THE STUDENT

To get the most out of this workbook, you should follow these suggestions:

1. Read the purpose of each exercise and make sure you understand the instructions before beginning work.

2. *Respect your participants' anonymity and do not breach confidentiality.* Do not include any information that could reveal a participant's identity to your instructor, teaching assistant, or other members of the class.

3. Be respectful of your participants. Explain to them that you are collecting data to assist you in a class project. Answer all of their questions. Explain the purpose of the project after you have collected your data. Take the opportunity to share your understanding of the topic with them.

4. Most research in sex and gender is based upon samples of middle-class college student participants. When you recruit volunteers to assist you in data collection, strive to obtain a diverse sample. Approach people who differ on factors such as age, race/ethnicity, education level, etc. Include these characteristics on your data sheet, and consider how these attributes may be related to your findings.

5. Use the questions that conclude each exercise to summarize your results. Compare and contrast your findings to the research from the text and class discussion and lecture. Consider what characteristics of your participants might have influenced your results.

CHAPTER 1

GENDER ROLES, GENDER STEREOTYPES, MASCULINITY, AND FEMININITY

PROJECT 1.1

CULTURAL IMAGES OF MEN AND WOMEN IN THE MEDIA

Purpose: The purpose of this exercise is to examine gender stereotypes as they are presented by the media.

Instructions: Collect six or more full-color magazine advertisements that contain photographic images of women and men. You should have a sufficient number of advertisements to provide you with six images of men and six images of women. Include at least one ad that portrays only men, one ad that portrays only women, and one or two ads that portray men and women together. Try to include as many diverse images of men and women as possible by including examples of women and men from different ethnic and racial groups and social classes.

1. How are women depicted in these advertisements? Describe similarities among the advertisements as well as differences.

2. How are men depicted in these advertisements? Describe similarities among the advertisements as well as differences.

3.   How do gender stereotypes vary by race, ethnicity, and social class? (If you had difficulty finding a diverse collection of photographs, you might want to comment on this fact.)

4.   How do men and women interact in these advertisements? Comment on factors such as touch, images of strength, dominance, sexuality, etc.

5.   What cues, if any, are present about sexual orientation? Describe.

6.   Reverse the positions of men and women in each advertisement. Do the messages about gender change? If so, how?

7.   What conclusions can you draw about how men and women are depicted in the media? How might these images relate to the development and maintenance of gender stereotypes?

PROJECT 1.2

THE COMPONENTS OF GENDER STEREOTYPES

Purpose: This exercise is designed to evaluate the components of people's stereotypes about women, men, masculinity, and femininity.

Instructions: Using the interview formats on the following pages, interview two men and two women. Select a variety of participants for this project. Include people who vary not only by sex but by other social categories (for example, age, race or ethnicity, sexual orientation, social class, etc.). Be sure to describe each participant by indicating her or his sex, age, and social attributes (for example, race or ethnicity, social class, etc.) at the top of each interview form.

Summarize your findings by answering the following questions.

1.   Did any of your respondents include personality traits (for example, independent, competitive, etc.) in their answers? If so, which personality traits?

2.   Did any of your respondents include role behaviors (for example, being the breadwinner, taking care of children) in their answers? If so, which role behaviors?

3.   Did any of your respondents include physical characteristics (for example, muscular, soft, etc.) in their answers? If so, which physical characteristics?

4. Relate your findings to the text's discussion of gender stereotypes and conceptions of masculinity and femininity. Compare and contrast your results to the research literature summarized in your text.

    Which results are similar? Can you suggest why?

    Which results are different? Can you suggest why?

5. Under what conditions might you have obtained different results?

Participant A

Sex _____   Age _____

Characteristics/Comments_____

1. Describe what comes to mind when you are asked to describe the typical woman.

2. Describe what comes to mind when you are asked to describe the typical man.

3. What makes a person feminine?

4. What makes a person masculine?

Participant B

Sex _____   Age   _____

Characteristics/Comments_____

1. Describe what comes to mind when you are asked to describe the typical woman.

2. Describe what comes to mind when you are asked to describe the typical man.

3. What makes a person feminine?

4. What makes a person masculine?

Participant C

Sex _____   Age _____

Characteristics/Comments_____

1. Describe what comes to mind when you are asked to describe the typical woman.

2. Describe what comes to mind when you are asked to describe the typical man.

3. What makes a person feminine?

4. What makes a person masculine?

Participant D

Sex _____   Age _____

Characteristics/Comments_____

1.   Describe what comes to mind when you are asked to describe the typical woman.

2.   Describe what comes to mind when you are asked to describe the typical man.

3.   What makes a person feminine?

4.   What makes a person masculine?

PROJECT 1.3

GENDER STEREOTYPES IN INTERACTION: RACE, SOCIAL CLASS, AGE, AND SEXUAL ORIENTATION

Purpose: The purpose of this exercise is to examine the manner in which gender stereotypes may differ as a function of social group.

Instructions: Gender stereotypes do not exist in isolation from other stereotypes. For example, stereotypes of masculinity might be more rigid than stereotypes of femininity because the value society places on the male role or because of heterosexist attitudes. People also hold stereotypes of their own and other ethnic and racial groups, social class (as defined by education level, income, and occupational status), age, and sexual orientation. Members of different social groups live under different conditions and may face different social expectations. In addition, gender stereotypes are strongly linked to aspects of physical appearance and sexuality. Thus, stereotypes of the "typical" woman or man may not generalize to members of other social groups.

For this exercise, select one social variable (that is, ethnicity or race, social class, age, or sexual orientation) that is of interest to you and that you suspect will interact with gender stereotypes. For example, you might wish to compare respondents' perceptions of a working-class man and woman, a lesbian and gay male, or an African-American man and woman.

Before you go out and collect your data, prepare the four data sheets that appear on the next four pages. Write a brief description of the target person to be evaluated by each of your participants. Half of the data sheets should describe a man and half of the data sheets should describe a woman. For example, two of your data sheets would describe an Asian heterosexual man and two of your data sheets would describe an Asian heterosexual women.

After you have prepared your data sheets, approach two men and two women and ask each to report his or her perceptions of one of the target persons. Be sure to describe each participant by indicating his or her sex, age, and social attributes (for example, race or ethnicity, social class, etc.) at the top of each interview form.

Participant A

Sex _____   Age _____

Characteristics/Comments_____

Think for a minute about the person described below.

Using the rating scale below, describe your impression of this person.

1.	1 Dependent	2	3	4	5	6	7 Independent
2.	1 Emotional	2	3	4	5	6	7 Unemotional
3.	1 Dominant	2	3	4	5	6	7 Passive
4.	1 Athletic	2	3	4	5	6	7 Not athletic
5.	1 Responsible	2	3	4	5	6	7 Irresponsible
6.	1 Soft-spoken	2	3	4	5	6	7 Loud-spoken
7.	1 Slim	2	3	4	5	6	7 Overweight
8.	1 Intelligent	2	3	4	5	6	7 Unintelligent
9.	1 Upper class	2	3	4	5	6	7 Lower class
10.	1 Lazy	2	3	4	5	6	7 Hard-working
11.	1 Family- oriented	2	3	4	5	6	7 Achievement- oriented

Participant B

Sex _____   Age _____

Characteristics/Comments_____

Think for a minute about the person described below.

Using the rating scale below, describe your impression of this person.

1.	1 Dependent	2	3	4	5	6	7 Independent
2.	1 Emotional	2	3	4	5	6	7 Unemotional
3.	1 Dominant	2	3	4	5	6	7 Passive
4.	1 Athletic	2	3	4	5	6	7 Not athletic
5.	1 Responsible	2	3	4	5	6	7 Irresponsible
6.	1 Soft-spoken	2	3	4	5	6	7 Loud-spoken
7.	1 Slim	2	3	4	5	6	7 Overweight
8.	1 Intelligent	2	3	4	5	6	7 Unintelligent
9.	1 Upper class	2	3	4	5	6	7 Lower class
10.	1 Lazy	2	3	4	5	6	7 Hard-working
11.	1 Family- oriented	2	3	4	5	6	7 Achievement- oriented

Participant C

Sex _____   Age _____

Characteristics/Comments_____

Think for a minute about the person described below.

Using the rating scale below, describe your impression of this person.

1.	1 Dependent	2	3	4	5	6	7 Independent
2.	1 Emotional	2	3	4	5	6	7 Unemotional
3.	1 Dominant	2	3	4	5	6	7 Passive
4.	1 Athletic	2	3	4	5	6	7 Not athletic
5.	1 Responsible	2	3	4	5	6	7 Irresponsible
6.	1 Soft-spoken	2	3	4	5	6	7 Loud-spoken
7.	1 Slim	2	3	4	5	6	7 Overweight
8.	1 Intelligent	2	3	4	5	6	7 Unintelligent
9.	1 Upper class	2	3	4	5	6	7 Lower class
10.	1 Lazy	2	3	4	5	6	7 Hard-working
11.	1 Family- oriented	2	3	4	5	6	7 Achievement- oriented

Participant D

Sex _____   Age _____

Characteristics/Comments_____

Think for a minute about the person described below.

Using the rating scale below, describe your impression of this person.

1.	1 Dependent	2	3	4	5	6	7 Independent
2.	1 Emotional	2	3	4	5	6	7 Unemotional
3.	1 Dominant	2	3	4	5	6	7 Passive
4.	1 Athletic	2	3	4	5	6	7 Not athletic
5.	1 Responsible	2	3	4	5	6	7 Irresponsible
6.	1 Soft-spoken	2	3	4	5	6	7 Loud-spoken
7.	1 Slim	2	3	4	5	6	7 Overweight
8.	1 Intelligent	2	3	4	5	6	7 Unintelligent
9.	1 Upper class	2	3	4	5	6	7 Lower class
10.	1 Lazy	2	3	4	5	6	7 Hard-working
11.	1 Family- oriented	2	3	4	5	6	7 Achievement- oriented

Summarize your data by responding to the following questions:

1. Compare and contrast your findings to the research on gender stereotypes reported in your text. In what ways do these perceptions overlap with stereotypes of femininity and masculinity? In what ways do they differ?

2. Gender stereotypes often interact with racism and heterosexism (anti-homosexual prejudice). Did you find any evidence for this? Explain.

3. Based on your findings, how similar are gender stereotypes across different groups?

Reference: Niemann, Yolanda F., Jennings, Leilani, Rozelle, Richard M., Baxter, James C., and Sullivan, Elroy. (1994). Use of free response and cluster analysis to determine stereotypes of eight groups. *Personality and Social Psychology Bulletin, 20*, 379–390.

PROJECT 1.4

GENDER ROLES: VIOLATING A NORM

Purpose: This exercise requires you to violate a norm associated with your gender role and evaluate the impact of this normative violation on yourself and others.

Instructions: Gender roles are comprised of a set of norms or expectations about behaviors that are appropriate for women or men. Norms may be *prescriptive* and specify what men or women should do in social situations. Norms also may be *descriptive* and indicate how women or men customarily behave in social situations.

In this exercise, you will identify some of the norms associated with your gender role and then violate a norm by behaving in a manner that deviates from the norm. Then, you will evaluate the results of this exercise through the series of questions that follow. A word of caution: Do not engage in any illegal or dangerous behavior or do anything that might cause you or others harm or acute embarrassment.

1. First, brainstorm. Generate a short list of behaviors that are more or less acceptable for each sex. This might include behaviors such as opening a door for another person, wearing cosmetics, paying the check at a restaurant, carrying a purse, comforting a crying child, wearing a football uniform and carrying a football helmet, etc.

2.   What is the norm associated with your gender role that you chose to violate? Why do you feel that this is a norm that is strongly tied to gender?

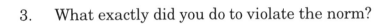

3.   What exactly did you do to violate the norm?

4.   How did violating this norm make you feel?

5.   How did other people react to your behavior? Did they try to restore gender role "normalcy"? If so, how?

6.   How did you respond to these reactions from other people?

7. How strong of an influence do you think gender roles have on behavior? Do you think this influence might vary across time and situations? If so, how?

PROJECT 1.5

FEMININITY, MASCULINITY, AND ANDROGYNY AS PSYCHOLOGICAL CONSTRUCTS

Purpose: The purpose of this exercise is to gain experience with and critique the Bem Sex Role Inventory (BSRI), a questionnaire that assesses masculinity and femininity.

Instructions: One of the most widely used personality trait measures is the Bem Sex Role Inventory (BSRI). This scale contains two independent subscales, one feminine and one masculine. Respondents indicate the extent to which each item is characteristic or descriptive of themselves. Sample items from the feminine and masculine subscales are listed below:

Feminine	Masculine
Compassionate	Assertive
Tender	Individualistic
Loves children	Defends own beliefs

Two scores are computed, one for the feminine subscale, one for the masculine subscale. Then respondents are characterized into one of the following four categories: *feminine* (high feminine score and low masculine score), *masculine* (low feminine score and high masculine score), *androgynous* (high feminine and masculine scores), or *undifferentiated* (low feminine and masculine scores).

1. How does Bem's multidimensional classification system differ from the unidimensional view of femininity and masculinity as bipolar opposites?

2. Sandra Bem identified items for the feminine and masculine subscales on the basis of social desirability. If an attribute was thought to be more desirable for a woman in American culture it was considered to be feminine. If an attribute was thought to be more desirable for a man in American culture it was thought to be masculine. The BSRI was first published in 1974. Do you think that lists of masculine and feminine attributes generated today in this manner might be different? How?

3. Generate a list of items describing attributes that you feel are desirable for women. Also make another list of desirable attributes for men. Are they different or similar? How do they compare with the items from the BSRI?

CHAPTER 2

RESEARCHING SEX AND GENDER

PROJECT 2.1

PRINCIPLES OF NONSEXIST RESEARCH

Purpose: In this exercise, you will be asked to critique a research design and apply the principles of nonsexist research.

Instructions: Read the description of the research study outlined in the paragraphs below. Next, analyze the study's methodology and assess how well it meets the principles of nonsexist research described in your text. Following your analysis and critique, redesign the study so that it meets the guidelines of nonsexist research.

Gender Differences in Codependency

A psychologist is interested in investigating gender differences in codependency. Based upon her counseling experience with husbands and wives of alcoholics, she is interested in studying how women and men become so involved in their spouses' drinking problems that it begins to affect their mental health and contributes to dysfunctional marital relationships. She predicts that men are more likely to be identified as alcoholics, and that male alcoholism is likely to be positively correlated with the degree of marital dysfunction as assessed by a clinical interview. Furthermore, she predicts that women will score higher on a measure of codependency that she has developed for the purpose of this study. This questionnaire contains three scales that measure the following variables that she feels are related to the concept of "enabling": (1) the extent to which the respondent obsessively talks about other people's problems, (2) the degree of dependency upon the marital partner, (3) the amount of responsibility assumed for the marital relationship, and (4) a standardized measure of self-esteem.

The psychologist recruits fifty married couples who are interested in serving as volunteers for this study through local support groups for people with troubled relationships and family members of alcoholics. After collecting her data, she finds a number of significant gender differences. As predicted, men are more likely to be identified as alcoholics, and women report higher relationship dependency and responsibility scores. No significant gender differences were found for self-esteem and talking about other people's problems. Moreover, alcoholism was found to be correlated with marital dysfunction (the correlation coefficient, +.60, was significant).

In her follow-up report, the psychologist makes the following conclusions:

1. There are significant gender differences in both alcoholism and codependency. Women are more likely to be the enablers in codependent relationships and men are more likely to be alcoholics.

2. Alcoholism causes dysfunctional marital relationships.

1. *Research topic:* In what ways might the choice of the research topic be biased? Are there cultural factors that might contribute to the legitimization of this topic? If so, which factors?

2. *Research question:* In what ways might sexist bias influence the definition of the research variables in this study? What biases may have influenced the definition of the research hypotheses?

3. *Research design:* What methodological problems exist in the research design? What demand characteristics might be present? Is the sampling (e.g., in terms of race, class, and sexual orientation) adequate? Are the measures appropriate? Are comparisons adequately drawn between groups?

4. *Analysis and interpretation of the data:* Are the gender differences interpreted and labeled appropriately? Do cultural biases enter into the interpretation of these findings?

5.   On this page, describe a nonsexist research design that addresses the criticisms you have identified in response to the previous questions.

PROJECT 2.2

INTERPRETING THE RESULTS OF RESEARCH IN SEX AND GENDER

Purpose: This exercise is designed to help you interpret and evaluate the results of experimental research.

Instructions: In general, experiments have an advantage over correlational studies because the researcher can assess the effects of the *independent variable* (the variable that is manipulated by the experimenter and distinguishes groups under study) on the *dependent variable* (the variable on which the two groups' mean scores differ). This becomes a problem in experiments that use sex as an independent variable. In these cases, participants are not randomly assigned to one of two groups, female versus male. Moreover, variables correlated with sex, such as differential socialization, status, etc., are not truly controlled in these instances. For this reason, the results of experimental research need to be interpreted with caution in order that significant differences might not be inappropriately attributed to biological sex differences.

On the other hand, correlational studies assess the degree to which naturally occurring variables are associated with each other. The exact nature of the relationships between two correlated variables may be difficult to tease out. If sex is found to be correlated with another variable this does not mean that being male or female caused this relationship. There always is the possibility that another unmeasured variable, also correlated with sex, is truly behind the observed relationship. Thus, correlational studies are unable to establish a causal relationship between variables.

Go to the campus library and find a journal article that reports social science research on sex and gender. Good choices are *Sex Roles, Journal of Social and Personality Psychology, Human Development, Child Development, Journal of Personality, Psychology of Women Quarterly, Journal of Family Issues, Journal of Marriage and the Family, Developmental Psychology, Journal of Sex Research,* etc. You might also refer to the reference list in your text for additional journals. Then, evaluate the article by answering the following questions. Be sure to attach a photocopy of the article to your worksheet.

1. Describe the study.

    What is the research hypothesis or hypotheses?

    What variables were studied?

    What are the characteristics of the sample?

    How were participants assigned to groups? What groups were studied?

2. Is this study an experimental or correlational study? Support your judgment with information provided in the article.

3.   Are significant group differences discussed in conjunction with group similarities? Provide evidence from the article.

4.   Has the researcher interpreted the statistical results appropriately? Are group differences discussed as sex-related differences or attributed to biological sex differences? Support your reasoning with evidence from the article.

5. Have the results of the study been generalized appropriately from the sample to other populations?

   To what populations were the results generalized?

   Was this appropriate? Why or why not?

Adapted from *Exploring/Teaching the Psychology of Women* (2nd ed.) by Michele A. Paludi by permission of the State University of New York Press. © 1996 State University of New York.

PROJECT 2.3

HETEROSEXISM IN RESEARCH:
THE HETEROSEXUAL QUESTIONNAIRE

Purpose: The purpose of this exercise is to examine the manner in which the use of heterosexual norms may bias the study of gay men's and lesbians' lives.

Instructions: Heterosexism is a form of bias in which heterosexual norms are used in studies of homosexual relationships. Gay men and lesbians are seen as deviating from a heterosexual norm, and this often leads to marginalization and pathologizing of their behavior.

Read the questionnaire below with this definition in mind. Then respond to the questions that follow.

1. What do you think caused your heterosexuality?

2. When and how did you first decide you were a heterosexual?

3. Is it possible that your heterosexuality is just a phase you may grow out of?

4. Is it possible that your heterosexuality stems from a neurotic fear of others of the same sex?

5. If you have never slept with a person of the same sex, is it possible that all you need is a good gay lover?

6. Do your parents know that you are straight? Do your friends and/or roommate(s) know? How did they react?

7. Why do you insist on flaunting your heterosexuality? Can't you just be who you are and keep it quiet?

8. Why do heterosexuals place so much emphasis on sex?

9. Why do heterosexuals feel compelled to seduce others into their lifestyle?

10. A disproportionate majority of child molesters are heterosexual. Do you consider it safe to expose children to heterosexual teachers?

11. Just what do men and women *do* in bed together? How can they truly know how to please each other, being so anatomically different?

12. With all the societal support marriage receives, the divorce rate is spiraling. Why are there so few stable relationships among heterosexuals?

13. Statistics show that lesbians have the lowest incidence of sexually transmitted diseases. Is it really safe for a woman to maintain a heterosexual lifestyle and run the risk of disease and pregnancy?

14. How can you become a whole person if you limit yourself to compulsive, exclusive heterosexuality?

15. Considering the menace of overpopulation, how could the human race survive if everyone were heterosexual?

16. Could you trust a heterosexual therapist to be objective? Don't you feel s/he might be inclined to influence you in the direction of her/his own leanings?

17. There seems to be very few happy heterosexuals. Techniques have been developed that might enable you to change if you really want to. Have you considered trying aversion therapy?

18. Would you want your child to be heterosexual, knowing the problems that s/he would face?

---

1. What were your first reactions upon reading this questionnaire?

2.   How does the wording of these questions influence the labeling of behaviors?

3.   How does the wording of these questions influence the interpretation of behaviors and differences?

4.   The author is parodying the assumptions underlying some questions that lesbians and gay men are asked about their sexual orientation. How might similar assumptions underlie research investigating biological and social factors in sexual orientation?

5.   Rewrite at least six of these questions to eliminate bias.

Reference: Rochlin, Martin. (1982, Spring). The heterosexual questionnaire. *M: Gentle men for gender justice / Changing men*, Issue #8. Reprinted by permission.

PROJECT 2.4

AN OBSERVATIONAL STUDY OF GENDER AND SOCIAL BEHAVIOR

Purpose: This exercise involves designing and conducting a naturalistic observation study. It also is designed to allow you to assess the extent to which naturalistic observation may be subject to observer bias.

Instructions: Naturalistic observation is a methodology that allows researchers the opportunity to record and describe behavior as it occurs outside the laboratory. This technique involves these steps: (1) identify the variable to be studied, (2) develop operational definitions of the actual behaviors to be studied, (3) choose a setting within which to observe these behaviors, and (4) observe and record the frequency with which the behaviors occur.

Naturalistic observation has an advantage over experimental studies in that behavior is observed (ideally) as it naturally occurs. On the other hand, a number of problems limit the conclusions one can draw from naturalistic observation of behavior. First, behavior might be rated differently by two observers depending upon whether they think they are observing a male or a female. This is especially true in the case of ambiguous behaviors, and precise operational definitions are necessary to reduce the problem of observer bias. Second, it is difficult to ascertain whether behavior in one setting might be generalizable to others. Thus, researchers must consider the effect the situation might have on people's behavior and consider testing this effect by conducting the research again in another setting.

1. First, identify the variable you want to study. Think about easily observed behaviors for which you might expect to find gender differences. For example, courtesy, playing with or caring for children, helping behaviors, aggressiveness in physical activities or sports, etc.

2. Develop one or more operational definitions for this variable. An operational definition clearly describes behavior in a form that is readily observable and measurable. For example, sports-related aggression might be operationalized as the number of tackles in a coed soccer game, or nurturance might be operationalized as the number of times a parent touches a child.

3. Describe the setting in which you have chosen to conduct your naturalistic observation. This might include settings such as a shopping mall, public park, etc.

4. Using the coding sheet below, record your data. Spend at least 90 minutes coding the frequency of behavior. Record the sex of the person performing the target behavior by making a hatch mark in the appropriate column (i.e., when a girl or woman performs the behavior, record the behavior in the "female" column; when a boy or man performs the behavior, record it in the "male" column).

Behavior	Female	Male

5. Summarize your data. Count the number of behaviors in each column. Compute the percentage of behaviors by gender by dividing the number of behaviors in each column by the total number of observations.

6. Interpret your data. Have you found gender differences or similarities? What are your conclusions?

7. Did you experience any difficulties in developing your operational definitions and using them to code behaviors? Did you observe any ambiguous behaviors that were difficult to code? If so, describe.

8. In what way(s) might the setting have affected the behaviors you observed?

9. Did you observe instances of observer bias in yourself? For example, if you saw a man perform a behavior typical of a woman did you ignore it, focus on it, or judge it?

10. What could you do to improve your study and overcome problems of bias?

PROJECT 2.5

NATURE VERSUS NURTURE IN THE NEWS

Purpose: The purpose of this exercise is to investigate the extent to which the news media consider the role of environment and heredity in reporting scientific research. Also, it is designed to encourage you to explore the nature of sex (physiological attributes) and gender (psychosocial attributes based on sex).

Instructions: Most social science researchers consider hard-and-fast positions on the "nature" (or genetic and biological factors) versus "nurture" (or environmental and social factors) debate to be overly simplistic. Sex and gender differences result from an *interaction* of biological and environmental factors. Rather than having unique effects, biology and the environment work together to influence human development and behavior. Media critics have argued that many stories of sex or gender differences reported in the popular media fail to provide an even-handed discussion of this interaction.

1. Locate at least three articles from the popular press that report sex or gender differences. Good sources are the local newspaper, *USA Today*, or popular magazines such as *Newsweek, Time, Self, Parenting*.

2. What *gender* differences are reported in these articles? Are these differences in the areas of social behavior or cognitive abilities, for instance?

3. What *sex* differences are reported in these articles? For example, do the articles focus on physiological differences in the brain or hormonal levels and functioning?

4. What causal explanations do the authors provide for these differences? Do they discuss biological factors such as genetic factors or hormonal levels? Do they discuss environmental factors such as differential socialization of boys and girls?

5. Evaluate these causal explanations. Do the authors consider both biological and environmental factors? Do the authors consider how biology and the environment interact in these cases?

CHAPTER 3

GENDER DIFFERENCES AND SIMILARITIES IN SOCIAL BEHAVIOR

PROJECT 3.1

BOYS WILL BE BOYS? AN OBSERVATIONAL STUDY OF CHILDREN'S ACTIVITY LEVELS

Purpose: This exercise is designed to have you assess factors that might influence differences in girls' and boys' activity levels.

Instructions: A thorough meta-analysis of the psychological research (Eaton & Enns, 1986) found that most studies find higher levels of physical activity among boys. Overall, this is considered to be a gender difference that is moderate in size.

A number of factors influence the size of this gender difference. These include the following:

Age: The size of this gender difference is smallest in infancy, and it increases during the preschool and elementary school years. This means that boys are more active than girls beginning the first year of life. In addition, compared to girls, boys' activity levels increase through middle childhood.

Presence of Peers: When children are playing alone, boys engage in more active play than do girls. On the other hand, when children are playing with their peers, the size of the gender difference increases. That is, compared to girls boys become even *more* active when they are playing with other children.

Spend about an hour observing preschool or elementary-school-aged children at play. Try to find one or more settings where children are interacting with minimal adult supervision. You might choose a setting such as a local park, a playground at a fast food restaurant, etc. Rather than code individual behaviors, try to get a sense of the boys' and girls' interactions. You will be asked to compare girls' and boys' activity levels when they are playing alone and when they are playing with at least one other peer.

You will first need to develop an operational definition of activity level that will enable you to evaluate the interactions. Keep it simple to reduce observer bias.

1. What sort of behaviors will you include in your observation? These might include rough-and-tumble play; loud, boisterous speech; quiet play; etc.

Summarize your observation by responding to the following questions.

2. Briefly describe the setting. What are the approximate ages of the children? Are the groups all girls, all boys, girls and boys? Are the children culturally diverse or homogeneous in terms of race or ethnicity?

3. Did the boys engage in more active play than the girls? Summarize your observation using the operational definitions you devised.

4. How did the situation influence the children's activity levels? Again, using your operational definitions, compare and contrast girls' and boys' activity levels when playing alone with their activity levels when playing with others.

5. Did you observe attempts to control behaviors or level of activity by adults or the children themselves? If so, describe.

6. Compare and contrast your observation with the research discussed in your text.

7. Boys are much more likely than girlsto be diagnosed as hyperactive. Considering the manner in which biological and social factors interact, what speculations might you make about this observed difference in hyperactivity?

Reference: Eaton, Warren O., & Enns, Lesley R. (1986). Sex differences in human motor activity level. *Psychological Bulletin, 100*, 19–28.

PROJECT 3.2

POPULAR CONCEPTIONS OF GENDER DIFFERENCES IN SOCIAL BEHAVIOR: HOW ARE MEN AND WOMEN DIFFERENT?

Purpose: This exercise is a replication of Swim's (1994) investigation of people's perceptions of the sizes of gender differences. Her study compared people's estimations of gender differences with the results of meta-analytic studies.

Instructions: Recruit two women and two men who are willing to complete a short questionnaire that assesses popular conceptions of the gender differences that have been studied by psychologists. Select a variety of participants for this project. Include four people who vary not only by sex but by other social categories (for example, age, race or ethnicity, sexual orientation, social class, etc.). Be sure to describe each participant by indicating her or his sex, age, and social attributes (for example, race or ethnicity, social class, etc.) at the top of each interview form.

Explain to your volunteers that the questionnaire contains descriptions of six traits or behaviors. Your participants should read each description and think about whether they believe men and women differ on each attribute. Then, they should provide their estimation of the size of the gender difference using this scale.

-3: Women are more likely than men to exhibit this trait or behavior. There is a large gender difference favoring women.

-2: Women are more likely than men to exhibit this trait or behavior. There is a moderate gender difference favoring women.

-1: Women are more likely than men to exhibit this trait or behavior. There is a small gender difference favoring women.

0: No difference. Women and men are equally likely to exhibit this trait or behavior.

+1: Men are more likely than women to exhibit this trait or behavior. There is a small gender difference favoring men.

+2: Men are more likely than women to exhibit this trait or behavior. There is a moderate gender difference favoring men.

+3: Men are more likely than women to exhibit this trait or behavior. There is a large gender difference favoring men.

Participant A

Sex _____   Age _____

Characteristics/Comments_____

Psychologists have studied whether men and women differ on each of the following behaviors or traits. In some cases large gender differences have been found. In others, small to no gender differences have been established. Read each of the following descriptions and provide your estimate of the degree to which women and men (as a group) differ on each trait or behavior.

1. *Leadership:* In groups composed of men and women, who is most likely to be selected as the leader? Men or women?

   Estimation of gender difference: _____

2. *Helping in the Presence of Others:* When a group of onlookers is present, who is most likely to assist someone in distress? Men or women?

   Estimation of gender difference: _____

3. *Helping When Alone:* In cases where someone needs assistance and no one else is around, who is most likely to help? Men or women?

   Estimation of gender difference: _____

4. *Aggression:* Are women or men more likely to be physically and verbally aggressive?

   Estimation of gender difference: _____

5. *Happiness:* Who is happier? Women or men?

   Estimation of gender difference: _____

6. *Influence by Group Pressure:* Conformity has been measured by a person's willingness to change their opinion when faced with opposing opinions held by other members in the group. Who is more likely to be influenced by group pressure to conform? Women or men?

   Estimation of gender difference: _____

Participant B

Sex _____   Age _____

Characteristics/Comments_____

Psychologists have studied whether men and women differ on each of the following behaviors or traits. In some cases large gender differences have been found. In others, small to no gender differences have been established. Read each of the following descriptions and provide your estimate of the degree to which women and men (as a group) differ on each trait or behavior.

1. *Leadership:* In groups composed of men and women, who is most likely to be selected as the leader? Men or women?

    Estimation of gender difference: _____

2. *Helping in the Presence of Others:* When a group of onlookers is present, who is most likely to assist someone in distress? Men or women?

    Estimation of gender difference: _____

3. *Helping When Alone:* In cases where someone needs assistance and no one else is around, who is most likely to help? Men or women?

    Estimation of gender difference: _____

4. *Aggression:* Are women or men more likely to be physically and verbally aggressive?

    Estimation of gender difference: _____

5. *Happiness:* Who is happier? Women or men?

    Estimation of gender difference: _____

6. *Influence by Group Pressure:* Conformity has been measured by a person's willingness to change their opinion when faced with opposing opinions held by other members in the group. Who is more likely to be influenced by group pressure to conform? Women or men?

    Estimation of gender difference: _____

Participant C

Sex _____   Age _____

Characteristics/Comments_____

Psychologists have studied whether men and women differ on each of the following behaviors or traits. In some cases large gender differences have been found. In others, small to no gender differences have been established. Read each of the following descriptions and provide your estimate of the degree to which women and men (as a group) differ on each trait or behavior.

1. *Leadership:* In groups composed of men and women, who is most likely to be selected as the leader? Men or women?

   Estimation of gender difference: _____

2. *Helping in the Presence of Others:* When a group of onlookers is present, who is most likely to assist someone in distress? Men or women?

   Estimation of gender difference: _____

3. *Helping When Alone:* In cases where someone needs assistance and no one else is around, who is most likely to help? Men or women?

   Estimation of gender difference: _____

4. *Aggression:* Are women or men more likely to be physically and verbally aggressive?

   Estimation of gender difference: _____

5. *Happiness:* Who is happier? Women or men?

   Estimation of gender difference: _____

6. *Influence by Group Pressure:* Conformity has been measured by a person's willingness to change their opinion when faced with opposing opinions held by other members in the group. Who is more likely to be influenced by group pressure to conform? Women or men?

   Estimation of gender difference: _____

Participant D

Sex _____   Age   _____

Characteristics/Comments_____

Psychologists have studied whether men and women differ on each of the following behaviors or traits. In some cases large gender differences have been found. In others, small to no gender differences have been established. Read each of the following descriptions and provide your estimate of the degree to which women and men (as a group) differ on each trait or behavior.

1. *Leadership:* In groups composed of men and women, who is most likely to be selected as the leader? Men or women?

    Estimation of gender difference: _____

2. *Helping in the Presence of Others:* When a group of onlookers is present, who is most likely to assist someone in distress? Men or women?

    Estimation of gender difference: _____

3. *Helping When Alone:* In cases where someone needs assistance and no one else is around, who is most likely to help? Men or women?

    Estimation of gender difference: _____

4. *Aggression:* Are women or men more likely to be physically and verbally aggressive?

    Estimation of gender difference: _____

5. *Happiness:* Who is happier? Women or men?

    Estimation of gender difference: _____

6. *Influence by Group Pressure:* Conformity has been measured by a person's willingness to change their opinion when faced with opposing opinions held by other members in the group. Who is more likely to be influenced by group pressure to conform? Women or men?

    Estimation of gender difference: _____

Summarize your results by answering the questions below.

1. Swim found that her college-student samples generally provided accurate estimations or underestimated gender differences. What were your findings?

2. One difference that was consistently overestimated was the gender difference in aggression (that is, men's aggressive tendencies were overestimated). Did you find similar results?

3. Swim suggested that the high level of accuracy exhibited in her sample might be due to the fact that it was composed of college students (aged 18 to 22) who might be likely to underestimate gender differences. Comment on this possibility, especially if your participants were not traditional college students.

4. What is the effect on others if people underestimate the impact of gender differences? If people downplay the role of gender in social behavior, what are the implications for women and men in social interaction?

Reference: Swim, Janet K. (1994). Perceived versus meta-analytic effect sizes: An assessment of the accuracy of gender stereotypes. *Journal of Personality and Social Psychology, 66*, 21–36.

PROJECT 3.3

SOCIALIZATION OF AGGRESSION: MODELING, REWARDS, AND PUNISHMENTS

Purpose: This exercise is designed to have you examine how differential social experiences of women and men may contribute to the observed gender difference in aggression.

Instructions: Gender differences in aggression are an excellent example of the interaction of biological and social influences on social behavior. Biological factors (for example, genetic and hormonal differences as well as differences in physical size) might predispose boys and men to be more aggressive. On the other hand, females and males have very different social experiences that interact with a possible biological predisposition to result in greater aggression among men and boys. Consider the messages, both implicit and explicit, you remember about aggression that you have encountered.

1. What messages did you receive about aggression from your parents, peers, or others. For example, how were you supposed to respond to a bully? Were you ever taught self-defense?

2. What messages did you receive about inhibiting aggression? For example, were you taught to walk away from a fight?

3.   Under what circumstances were you punished for being aggressive?
     Under what circumstances were you rewarded for being aggressive?

4.   Evaluate the effect of your experiences on the socialization of aggression.
     How might these factors contribute to the expression of direct aggression
     (i.e., physical force). How might these factors contribute to the expression
     of indirect aggression (i.e., talking behind someone's back)?

5.   In what ways might these factors be related to the inhibition of
     aggression?

PROJECT 3.4

GILLIGAN'S MODEL OF MORAL REASONING

Purpose: The purpose of this exercise is to compare the use of justice and care orientations in moral reasoning. The exercise utilizes the methodology developed by Ford and Lowery (1986) in their study of gender and moral reasoning.

Instructions: Psychologist Carol Gilligan (1982) presented a unique perspective on the relationship between gender and moral reasoning. She identified two perspectives, one focused on care and another focused on justice, that both men and women use in making moral judgments.

Care Perspective: This perspective emphasizes the interrelatedness of people and their relationships. From this perspective, moral judgments involve considering the needs of others who are dependent upon you, avoiding causing hurt, sensitivity to others and their needs, and the necessity of meeting one's responsibilities in relationships. Moral decisions are usually conceptualized in terms of maintaining relationships to others.

Justice Perspective: This perspective emphasizes principles of reciprocity that are based on contractual obligations between others. From this perspective judgments involve the negotiation of impartial principles or standards. Moral decisions based upon the evaluation of whether standards of fairness or commitment have been upheld are characteristic of this perspective.

Because psychological development is not the same for women and men, Gilligan expected gender differences in the use of these two perspectives. Because women's developmental issues center around attachment, women would be more likely to emphasize the care orientation. In contrast, men's concern with separation and individuation would make them more likely to emphasize the justice orientation.

Gilligan's model, especially her predictions about gender differences, have aroused considerable controversy. Evidence for gender differences has been inconsistent. On the other hand, her contention that the care perspective is an important element in people's moral judgments may be less controversial.

How prevalent are these two perspectives in people's moral reasoning? The questions on the following worksheets ask you to evaluate these two perspectives within the context of your own experience. First, consider three important dilemmas from your past. These incidents should involve consideration of competing needs, desires, rights, and obligations of other people. After you have completed the worksheets, evaluate your work by responding to the questions that follow.

1.   Conflict #1: Describe the dilemma briefly in the space below:

2.   Approximately how old were you at the time?

3.   How important did this dilemma seem to be at that time? (circle one)

1	2	3	4	5	6	7
Not at all important						Extremely important

4.   How difficult was it for you to decide what to do? (circle one)

1	2	3	4	5	6	7
Not at all difficult						Extremely difficult

5.   To what extent did you utilize the care perspective in resolving this dilemma? (circle one)

1	2	3	4	5	6	7
Not at all						A great deal

6.   To what extent did you utilize the justice perspective in resolving this dilemma? (circle one)

1	2	3	4	5	6	7
Not at all						A great deal

1.   Conflict #2: Describe the dilemma briefly in the space below:

2.   Approximately how old were you at the time?

3.   How important did this dilemma seem to be at that time? (circle one)

      1   2   3   4   5   6   7
Not at all   Extremely
important   important

4.   How difficult was it for you to decide what to do? (circle one)

      1   2   3   4   5   6   7
Not at all   Extremely
  difficult   difficult

5.   To what extent did you utilize the care perspective in resolving this
      dilemma? (circle one)

      1   2   3   4   5   6   7
Not at all   A great deal

6.   To what extent did you utilize the justice perspective in resolving this
      dilemma? (circle one)

      1   2   3   4   5   6   7
Not at all   A great deal

1. Conflict #3: Describe the dilemma briefly in the space below:

2. Approximately how old were you at the time?

3. How important did this dilemma seem to be at that time? (circle one)

1	2	3	4	5	6	7
Not at all important						Extremely important

4. How difficult was it for you to decide what to do? (circle one)

1	2	3	4	5	6	7
Not at all difficult						Extremely difficult

5. To what extent did you utilize the care perspective in resolving this dilemma? (circle one)

1	2	3	4	5	6	7
Not at all						A great deal

6. To what extent did you utilize the justice perspective in resolving this dilemma? (circle one)

1	2	3	4	5	6	7
Not at all						A great deal

1. Did you use the justice perspective or the care perspective consistently? Was the justice perspective or the care perspective used in resolving some dilemmas but not others?

2. Were your importance and difficulty ratings related to the extent to which you utilized the care perspective? The justice perspective?

3.   What do you think about the possibility of gender differences in moral reasoning? Do you think they might be related to gender roles, life stage, or age, for example? Support your conclusions by reference to your worksheets and to your text.

References: Ford, Maureen R., & Lowery, Carol R. (1986). Gender differences in moral reasoning: A comparison of the use of justice and care orientations. *Journal of Personality and Social Psychology, 50,* 777–783.

Gilligan, Carol (1982). *In a different voice: Psychological theory and women's development.* Cambridge, MA: Harvard University Press.

CHAPTER 4

GENDER AND LANGUAGE

PROJECT 4.1

GENDER AND NONVERBAL BEHAVIOR

Purpose: The purpose of this exercise is to examine gender differences and similarities in nonverbal behavior.

Instructions: Observe three dyads (two men, two women, and one woman and one man) that you find interacting in a social setting. Large public places such as public parks, fitness clubs, cafeterias, the university quad, etc., are good locations because it is more likely that you will be able to observe the interactions for an adequate period of time without being obvious or intrusive.

Situate yourself where you can see the faces of both participants in each dyad. Using the data sheets on the following pages, analyze the nonverbal behavior in each interaction using the variables and operational definitions below.

Participants: Describe the people you observe. Record their age, sex, and ethnicity. Also, record any other information that you think might affect their interaction. This might include the nature of their relationship (if you happen to know the participants), social status (e.g., an authority figure such as a parent or teacher would be higher in status compared to a child or student).

Setting: Briefly describe the setting. Comment on where you made your observations, the time of day, whether the participants are sitting or standing, and any other factors that you think are important. Record the length of time you observe the dyad.

Touch: Count the number of times each person in the dyad touches the other. Record with hatch marks the number of times Person A touches Person B and the number of times Person B touches Person A.

Smiling: Record the amount of smiling by using the two rating scales on the data sheet. First, rate the amount of smiles exchanged during the interaction. Then, summarize the pattern of smiles exchanged by the participants.

Eye Contact: Record the amount of eye contact by using the rating scale on the data sheet. Evaluate the proportion of time each individual spends gazing into the other's eyes.

Interpersonal Distance: Make an estimation of the distance between the bodies of the two individuals in each dyad. Approximately how much personal space do they maintain during the interaction? Who moves closer to whom? Who moves away?

Dyad 1

Person A: Sex_____   Race/Ethnicity_____

Person B: Sex_____   Race/Ethnicity_____

Comments:_____

Setting:_____

Length of Observation: _____ minutes

Frequency of Touch

Person A touches Person B   _____

Person B touches Person A   _____

Smiling

1	2	3	4	5	6	7
Infrequent						Frequent

1	2	3	4	5	6	7
Person A smiles more			Equal smiles			Person B smiles more

Eye Contact

1	2	3	4	5	6	7
Person A gazes more			Equal eye contact			Person B gazes more

Interpersonal Distance

Dyad 2

Person A: Sex_____   Race/Ethnicity_____

Person B: Sex_____   Race/Ethnicity_____

Comments:_____

Setting:_____

Length of Observation: _____ minutes

Frequency of Touch

Person A touches Person B   _____

Person B touches Person A   _____

Smiling

1	2	3	4	5	6	7
Infrequent						Frequent

1	2	3	4	5	6	7
Person A smiles more			Equal smiles			Person B smiles more

Eye Contact

1	2	3	4	5	6	7
Person A gazes more			Equal eye contact			Person B gazes more

Interpersonal Distance

Dyad 3

Person A: Sex_____   Race/Ethnicity_____

Person B: Sex_____   Race/Ethnicity_____

Comments:_____

Setting:_____

Length of Observation: _____ minutes

Frequency of Touch

Person A touches Person B   _____

Person B touches Person A   _____

Smiling

1	2	3	4	5	6	7
Infrequent						Frequent

1	2	3	4	5	6	7
Person A smiles more			Equal smiles			Person B smiles more

Eye Contact

1	2	3	4	5	6	7
Person A gazes more			Equal eye contact			Person B gazes more

Interpersonal Distance

Summarize your results by responding to the following questions.

1.   Compare the nonverbal behaviors of the men and women you observed. Describe similarities as well as differences.

2.   Compare and contrast the nonverbal behaviors you observed in the same-sex and female-male dyads.

3.   Relate your findings to the course material on gender, race and ethnicity, and nonverbal behavior. Compare and contrast your results to the research literature summarized in your text.

Which results are similar? Can you suggest why?

Which results are different? Can you suggest why?

4.   Many researchers (e.g., Henley, 1977) interpret gender differences in nonverbal behavior within the context of power and status differences between men and women. Comment on this interpretation, using your data and your text to support your position.

Reference: Henley, Nancy. (1977). *Body politics: Power, sex, and nonverbal communication.* Englewood Cliffs, NJ: Prentice-Hall.

PROJECT 4.2

GENDER AND CONVERSATIONAL PATTERNS

Purpose: The purpose of this exercise is to evaluate the results of research investigating how men and women differ in their language usage.

Instructions: For this project you will need a tape recorder and the cooperation of your friends. Recruit two friends, one female and one male, to agree to have you tape record a staged discussion for which you provide the topic. Do not tape record any conversation without the permission of the people involved.

Using the data sheet on the following page, analyze the conversational patterns in each interaction using the variables and operational definitions below.

Participants: Describe the people you observe. Record their sex and ethnicity. Also record any other information that you think might affect their interaction (for example, relationships, status, etc.).

Setting: Briefly describe the setting. Comment on where you made your observations, the time of day, whether the participants are sitting or standing, and any other factors that you think are important. Record the length of time you observe the dyad.

Time Speaking: Record the amount of time each person speaks.

Interruptions: A speaker might be interrupted in two ways. A conversational topic that is introduced by a speaker might not be picked up by the listener; thus it is "dropped". In other cases, a speaker might be unable to complete a statement because the listener interjects comments or changes the topic.

Tag Questions: This linguistic construction includes a statement that is modified by appending a question at the end that encourages a response from the listener. "It's a nice day, isn't it?" "Gail and Lee performed that operation beautifully, didn't they?"

Supportive Remarks: These include brief remarks and comments that indicate attentiveness to and interest in the speaker, such as "mmm-hmm" or "that's right".

Tentative Comments: This involves the use of disclaimers or hedges. Disclaimers communicate uncertainty (such as "I'm not sure, but it seems to me"). Hedges include comments such as "kinda like", "I don't know, but", and "I guess".

Conversational Patterns Data Sheet

Person A: Sex_____   Race/Ethnicity_____

Person B: Sex_____   Race/Ethnicity_____

Comments:_____

Setting:_____

Length of Observation: _____ minutes

Time Speaking

      Person A _____   Person B _____

Number of Interruptions

      Person A interrupts Person B _____

      Person B interrupts Person A _____

Number of Tag Questions

      Person A _____   Person B _____

Number of Supportive Remarks

      Person A _____   Person B _____

Number of Tentative Comments

      Person A _____   Person B _____

Summarize your results by responding to the following questions.

1. Compare the conversational patterns of the woman and man you observed. Describe similarities as well as differences.

2. Relate your findings to the text's discussion of gender, race and ethnicity, and language use. Compare and contrast your results to the research literature summarized in your text.

    Which results are similar? Can you suggest why?

    Which results are different? Can you suggest why?

3.   One interpretation of the research is that gender differences in language use are related to differences in status and power (Henley, 1977). Others interpret these differences as reflecting differences in social roles (Wood, 1994). That is, women are more likely to use conversational styles that are interpersonally warm and supportive of others. Comment on these interpretations, using your data and your text to support your argument.

References: Henley, Nancy. (1977). *Body politics: Power, sex, and nonverbal communication.* Englewood Cliffs, NJ: Prentice-Hall.

Wood, Julia. T. (1994). *Gendered lives: Communication, gender, and culture.* Belmont, CA: Wadsworth.

PROJECT 4.3

SEXIST LANGUAGE AND COGNITION

Purpose: This exercise examines the effect of gendered language on people's thought processes. It is based upon Moulton, Robinson, & Elias's (1978) study that investigated the effect of the use of the masculine as a generic pronoun.

Instructions: For this project you will need to select three adults who are willing to spend approximately five minutes writing a brief paragraph for you. Your volunteers should be approximately the same age.

Using the data sheets on the following pages, ask each volunteer to complete the descriptive information at the top of the sheet. Then have each person read the stimulus sentences and write a short paragraph that develops these sentences into a brief story.

Three versions of the data sheet have been prepared. The same sentences appear on each, but you will notice that the pronoun has been manipulated in each version. One sentence contains the masculine pronoun (*his*), one the plural (*their*), and the third contains both (*his or her*). Each volunteer will read only one version.

After your volunteers have written their paragraphs, explain the purpose of the exercise. Moulton and her colleagues found that when the masculine pronoun was used as a generic pronoun (that is, to refer to both women and men), their college student participants were significantly more likely to think of men. They concluded that gendered language can bias cognitive processes. Be sure to answer any questions your participants might have.

After you have collected your data, summarize your results by answering the questions at the end of this project.

Creative Writing Exercise

Sex _____   Age _____

Many residential college students have never lived away from home before. In these cases, the homesick student will call home frequently to maintain contact with his family and friends.

Creative Writing Exercise

Sex _____   Age   _____

Many residential college students have never lived away from home before. In these cases, the homesick student will call home frequently to maintain contact with his or her family and friends.

Creative Writing Exercise

Sex _____   Age _____

Many residential college students have never lived away from home before. In these cases, homesick students will call home frequently to maintain contact with their family and friends.

1.   Compare the three stories. How many were about men? How many were about women?

2.   Were your results consistent with the research? Compare and contrast your findings with the research discussed in this project and in your text.

3.   This classic study was conducted over 20 years ago. Do you think that people have become more sensitive to the use of gendered pronouns and sexist language? Why or why not?

Reference: Moulton, Janice. R., Robinson, G. M., & Elias, Cherin. (1978). Psychology in action: Sex bias in language use: "Neutral" pronouns that aren't. *American Psychologist, 33,* 1032–1036.

PROJECT 4.4

USING NONSEXIST LANGUAGE

Purpose: This exercise is an opportunity to practice using nonsexist language. It also is designed to help you explore the effect of gendered terms on the perceptions of other people.

Instructions: Proponents of the use of nonsexist language point to the reciprocal relationship between language and thought. Just as our language reflects what we know about men and women, it also may shape how we think about men and women. A particular problem is that gendered terms often have connotations (implicit meanings) that differ when they are applied to women and men.

Nonsexist language attempts to avoid a number of psycholinguistic problems. These include the following:

Male as Normative: Many linguistic constructions in the English language are androcentric in nature. This involves the use of terms such as *man* or *mankind* to refer to both men and women and the use of the masculine pronoun to refer to both sexes. Corrections include substituting the term *person* for *man,* such as referring to the chairperson of a committee rather than the chairman. Other corrections might involve considerable reconstruction of the term. Examples include the substitution of the term *first-year student* in place of *freshman* or *sewer access cover* to replace *manhole cover.*

Infantilization: This involves the use of euphemisms to refer to women (and sometimes people of color, gay men, and lesbians) that connotes dependency and immaturity. This includes referring to women as *girls* or *chicks* or gay men as *mama's boys* and *sissies.*

Parallel Words: Another linguistic category includes words that have a neutral or positive connotation in reference to men. When the parallel term refers to women, however, the connotation becomes sexualized or negative. The classic example is *master,* which connotes strength and competence. The parallel word, *mistress,* is not truly equivalent, for it refers to a woman who is sexually involved with a man for financial gain.

Revise each of the terms on the worksheet that follows to meet the guidelines of nonsexist language. Then respond to the questions that follow.

Penmanship   _____

Master craftsman   _____

Manmade   _____

Housewife   _____

Girl Friday   _____

Cover girl   _____

Right-hand man   _____

Cowboy   _____

Sportsmanship   _____

Mother tongue   _____

Forefathers   _____

Man about town   _____

Coed   _____

Gentlemen's agreement   _____

Jack of all trades   _____

Majorette   _____

First Lady   _____

One-up-man-ship   _____

Self-made man   _____

Mastermind   _____

Tomboy   _____

Bachelor's degree   _____

Middleman   _____

Showmanship   _____

1. Were some terms more difficult to revise than others? Which ones? Why?

2. Did the revised versions of some terms change the connotation more than others? Which ones? Why?

Adapted from Paludi, Michele A. Nonsexist language usage. In Vivian P. Makosky et al. (Eds.), *Activities handbook for the teaching of psychology* (Vol. 3) (pp. 318–319). Washington, DC: American Psychological Association. Copyright © 1990 by the American Psychological Association. Adapted with permission.

PROJECT 4.5

POPULAR CONCEPTIONS OF GENDER DIFFERENCES IN NONVERBAL BEHAVIOR: HOW ARE MEN AND WOMEN DIFFERENT?

Purpose: This exercise is another replication of Swim's (1994) investigation of people's perceptions of the sizes of gender differences compared with the results of meta-analytic studies.

Instructions: Recruit two men and two women who are willing to complete a short questionnaire that assesses popular conceptions of the gender differences that have been studied by psychologists. Select a variety of participants for this project. Include four people who vary not only by sex but by other social categories (for example, age, race or ethnicity, sexual orientation, social class, etc.). Be sure to describe each participant by indicating his or her sex, age, and social attributes (for example, race or ethnicity, social class, etc.) at the top of each interview form.

Explain to your volunteers that the questionnaire contains descriptions of four traits or behaviors. Your participants should read the descriptions and think about whether they believe men and women differ on each attribute. Then, they should provide their estimation of the size of the gender difference using this scale.

-3: Women are more likely than men to exhibit this trait or behavior. There is a large gender difference favoring women.

-2: Women are more likely than men to exhibit this trait or behavior. There is a moderate gender difference favoring women.

-1: Women are more likely than men to exhibit this trait or behavior. There is a small gender difference favoring women.

0: No difference. Women and men are equally likely to exhibit this trait or behavior.

+1: Men are more likely than women to exhibit this trait or behavior. There is a small gender difference favoring men.

+2: Men are more likely than women to exhibit this trait or behavior. There is a moderate gender difference favoring men.

+3: Men are more likely than women to exhibit this trait or behavior. There is a large gender difference favoring men.

Participant A

Sex _____   Age _____

Characteristics/Comments_____

Psychologists have studied whether men and women differ on each of the following behaviors or traits. In some cases large gender differences have been found. In others, small to no gender differences have been established. Read each of the following descriptions and provide your estimate of the degree to which women and men (as a group) differ on each trait or behavior.

1. *Nonverbal Decoding:* This involves the ability to read or interpret the emotional expressions of others. Who is better at interpreting nonverbal cues? Men or women?

    Estimation of gender difference: _____

2. *Maintaining Eye Contact:* When two or more people are engaged in a conversation, who is most likely to gaze intently? Women or men?

    Estimation of gender difference: _____

3. *Agitation and Restless Behavior:* Who is more likely to fidget, change position, and act restless in a conversation? Men or women?

    Estimation of gender difference: _____

4. *Communication of Encouragement and Involvement:* Who is more likely to communicate encouragement and involvement through gestures such as a forward lean, nodding, etc.? Women or men?

    Estimation of gender difference: _____

Participant B

Sex _____   Age   _____

Characteristics/Comments_____

Psychologists have studied whether men and women differ on each of the following behaviors or traits. In some cases large gender differences have been found. In others, small to no gender differences have been established. Read each of the following descriptions and provide your estimate of the degree to which women and men (as a group) differ on each trait or behavior.

1. *Nonverbal Decoding:* This involves the ability to read or interpret the emotional expressions of others. Who is better at interpreting nonverbal cues? Men or women?

    Estimation of gender difference: _____

2. *Maintaining Eye Contact:* When two or more people are engaged in a conversation, who is most likely to gaze intently? Women or men?

    Estimation of gender difference: _____

3. *Agitation and Restless Behavior:* Who is more likely to fidget, change position, and act restless in a conversation? Men or women?

    Estimation of gender difference: _____

4. *Communication of Encouragement and Involvement:* Who is more likely to communicate encouragement and involvement through gestures such as a forward lean, nodding, etc.? Women or men?

    Estimation of gender difference: _____

Participant C

Sex _____   Age _____

Characteristics/Comments_____

Psychologists have studied whether men and women differ on each of the following behaviors or traits. In some cases large gender differences have been found. In others, small to no gender differences have been established. Read each of the following descriptions and provide your estimate of the degree to which women and men (as a group) differ on each trait or behavior.

1. *Nonverbal Decoding:* This involves the ability to read or interpret the emotional expressions of others. Who is better at interpreting nonverbal cues? Men or women?

    Estimation of gender difference: _____

2. *Maintaining Eye Contact:* When two or more people are engaged in a conversation, who is most likely to gaze intently? Women or men?

    Estimation of gender difference: _____

3. *Agitation and Restless Behavior:* Who is more likely to fidget, change position, and act restless in a conversation? Men or women?

    Estimation of gender difference: _____

4. *Communication of Encouragement and Involvement:* Who is more likely to communicate encouragement and involvement through gestures such as a forward lean, nodding, etc.? Women or men?

    Estimation of gender difference: _____

Participant D

Sex _____   Age _____

Characteristics/Comments_____

Psychologists have studied whether men and women differ on each of the following behaviors or traits. In some cases large gender differences have been found. In others, small to no gender differences have been established. Read each of the following descriptions and provide your estimate of the degree to which women and men (as a group) differ on each trait or behavior.

1. *Nonverbal Decoding:* This involves the ability to read or interpret the emotional expressions of others. Who is better at interpreting nonverbal cues? Men or women?

    Estimation of gender difference: _____

2. *Maintaining Eye Contact:* When two or more people are engaged in a conversation, who is most likely to gaze intently? Women or men?

    Estimation of gender difference: _____

3. *Agitation and Restless Behavior:* Who is more likely to fidget, change position, and act restless in a conversation? Men or women?

    Estimation of gender difference: _____

4. *Communication of Encouragement and Involvement:* Who is more likely to communicate encouragement and involvement through gestures such as a forward lean, nodding, etc.? Women or men?

    Estimation of gender difference: _____

Summarize your results by answering the questions below.

1. Swim found that her college-student samples generally provided accurate estimations or underestimated gender differences. What were your findings?

2. Swim suggested that the high level of accuracy exhibited in her sample might be due to the fact that it was composed of college students (aged 18 to 22) who might be likely to underestimate gender differences. Comment on this possibility, especially if your participants were not traditional college students.

3. What is the effect on others if people underestimate the impact of gender differences? If people downplay the role of gender in social behavior, what are the implications for men and women in social interaction?

Reference: Swim, Janet K. (1994). Perceived versus meta-analytic effect sizes: An assessment of the accuracy of gender stereotypes. *Journal of Personality and Social Psychology, 66,* 21–36.

CHAPTER 5

GENDER IDENTITY DEVELOPMENT

PROJECT 5.1

GENDER STEREOTYPES AND ADULT EXPECTATIONS FOR INFANTS: A CONTENT ANALYSIS OF BIRTH CONGRATULATIONS CARDS

Purpose: This exercise is a partial replication of a study conducted by Judith Bridges (1993). It is designed to examine gender stereotypes of infants as represented in greeting cards.

Instructions: Research has consistently shown that gender-role socialization begins in infancy. Adults' expectations about gender-typed interests, attributes, and attitudes as well as gender-role stereotypes may be communicated in many ways.

For this project you will need to visit a store that sells congratulations cards for parents of newborns. Try to identify a location that carries a large selection of cards (for example, a well-stocked grocery store, a specialty card store in a mall, or a discount department store). Aim for a location that serves a diverse group of shoppers. Try to locate at least twenty cards.

Decide whether each card is to be sent to the parents of a boy or a girl. Using the data sheet on the following page, analyze the color, layout, and text of the cards according to the coding system outlined below. Indicate the number of cards for girls and boys that can be represented by each category.

Color of Card: Code the predominant color of the card. If you were to characterize the card by choosing one color, what would it be?

Images of Toys: What is on the cover of the card? If toys are depicted on the cover, code the type of toy. Code as sports equipment toys such as balls and bats. Action toys include pull toys, vehicles, shovels, etc. Infant toys include things that are specific to newborns such as rattles and pacifiers.

Clothing Decorations: Assess whether the cover of the card includes images of decorative clothing items that are characterized by such things as ribbons, bows, lace (i.e., frilliness), or hearts. Also indicate whether clothing is decorated with more functional patterns such as geometric patterns, stripes, or plaids.

Description of Infant's Attributes: Read the text of the card. If it refers to the infant as sweet, precious, or cute, code these variables.

After collecting your data, summarize your results by responding to the questions that follow.

Congratulations Cards Coding Sheet

	Girls	Boys
Color		
Pink		
Blue		
Mixed/Other		
Images of Toys		
Stuffed Animal		
Sports Equipment		
Action Toy		
Infant Toy		
Clothing Decorations		
Frilliness		
Flowers		
Hearts		
Plaids/Stripes		
Geometric Shapes		
Description of Infant's Attributes		
Sweet		
Precious		
Cute		
Other		

1. Bridges concluded that she identified a significant difference in stereotypes of infants. Boys' cards were more likely to be blue and depict physical activity and functional clothing. Girls' cards were more likely to be pink, depict frilly clothing, and refer to the infant's feminine personality attributes. Compare and contrast your results with these findings.

2. Consider the research in your text about the role adults' stereotypes play in socializing infants and children to gender roles. What beliefs are communicated in these cards?

3. Suppose you were buying a congratulations card following the birth of a niece or nephew. What sort of card would you look for? Why?

Reference: Bridges, Judith S. (1993). Pink or blue: Gender-stereotypic perceptions of infants as conveyed by birth congratulations cards. *Psychology of Women Quarterly*, *17*, 193–205.

PROJECT 5.2

MESSAGES FROM CHILDHOOD ABOUT SEX AND GENDER: AN AUTOBIOGRAPHICAL EXERCISE

Purpose: This exercise is designed to encourage you to consider the messages about sex and gender you received during childhood and relate them to the theory and research in your text.

Instructions: Consider important events or influences during your childhood that you feel have influenced your gender identity development. Consider the messages you received about sex and gender from important people (for example, parents, teachers, peers, role models) or factors such as the media, the educational system, etc. Because there are considerable variations in gender-role socialization across social groups, consider as well the influence of any other salient factors (for example, your race or ethnicity, the historical-cultural period during which you grew up, your sexual orientation, etc.).

1. What were you told big boys should be like? What were you told big girls should be like?

2. What were tomboys like? What were sissies like?

3.   What types of games did you play with your friends?

4.   Did you participate in physical education classes or organized sports (like Little League or AYSO)? If so, did you enjoy this experience? Why or why not?

5. What were your responsibilities in your family? What were your chores? Did you do yard work, housework, babysitting?

6. What did you want to be when you grew up? Why? What are your occupational goals today?

7.   Do you think these experiences influenced the development of your gender identity? How? Integrate your experience with the material in your text. Which of your experiences are consistent with the theory and research reported in the text? How do they differ?

PROJECT 5.3

GENDER AND INTERACTIONS WITH PEERS : AN OBSERVATIONAL PROJECT

Purpose: This exercise requires you to examine gender differences and similarities in children's play patterns and interactions with their peers.

Instructions: Spend about an hour observing preschool or elementary-school-aged children at play. Try to find a setting where children are interacting with minimal adult supervision. An organized soccer game, for example, would not be appropriate for this project. Rather than code individual behaviors, try to get a sense of the boys' and girls' interactions. Summarize your observation by responding to the questions below.

1. Briefly describe the setting. What are the approximate ages of the children? Is the group culturally diverse or homogeneous in terms of race or ethnicity? Are the children paying in all-male, all-female, or mixed-gender groups?

2. How physically active are the boys? The girls? Are any children engaging in rough-and-tumble play? Which ones? Are any children engaging in cooperative play? Which ones?

3. What sorts of activities are the children engaged in? Do you observe gender differences or similarities?

4. Comment on the degree of gender segregation you observe.

5. If you observe any disputes, how do the children settle them? Do you observe any differences between the girls and the boys?

PROJECT 5.4

GENDER DIFFERENCES AND SIMILARITIES IN CHILDHOOD AND ADOLESCENT FRIENDSHIPS

Purpose: This exercise is designed to evaluate the nature of boys' and girls' friendships in childhood and adolescence.

Instructions: Using the data sheets on the following pages, interview two boys and two girls about their friends and their understanding of friendship. One boy and one girl should be elementary school age (approximately 6 to 12 years), and one girl-boy pair should be adolescent. Be sure to describe each participant by indicating his or her sex, age, and social attributes (for example, race or ethnicity or social class) at the top of the interview forms.

Then, summarize your findings by answering the following questions.

1. Compare and contrast your participants' responses to the research discussed in the text. Do your findings support the research findings? How? Are any responses inconsistent with the research? How would you explain this?

2. What do you conclude? How are boys' and girls' friendships similar? How do they differ?

3. How do girls' and boys' friendships differ as a function of age?

4. How would you have responded to these questions at roughly the same ages?

Participant A

Sex _____   Age _____

Characteristics/Comments_____

1.   What do you do with your friends?

2.   Do you have a best friend? Who is s/he? What is your best friend like?

3.   Why is this person your best friend?

Participant B

Sex _____   Age   _____

Characteristics/Comments_____

1.   What do you do with your friends?

2.   Do you have a best friend? Who is s/he? What is your best friend like?

3.   Why is this person your best friend?

Participant C

Sex _____   Age _____

Characteristics/Comments_____

1.   What do you do with your friends?

2.   Do you have a best friend? Who is s/he? What is your best friend like?

3.   Why is this person your best friend?

Participant D

Sex _____   Age _____

Characteristics/Comments_____

1.   What do you do with your friends?

2.   Do you have a best friend? Who is s/he? What is your best friend like?

3.   Why is this person your best friend?

PROJECT 5.5

CULTURAL MESSAGES ABOUT GENDER ROLES: AN ANALYSIS OF CHILDREN'S MEDIA

Purpose: The purpose of this exercise is to evaluate the extent to which children's television programming contains gender-stereotypic messages.

Instructions: Because children spend a large proportion of their day watching television, children's programming is an important socializing agent. A number of researchers and media critics have pointed to the pervasiveness of gender stereotyping in children's cartoons and other television programs.

Spend an hour or two watching children's cartoons or family-oriented programs. Analyze the programming according to the following criteria:

Commercial Narrators: Count and then compute the percentage of male and female narrators. Include voice-over (audio only) narration as well as audio-video narration.

Program Characters: Count and then compute the percentage of female and male characters. If the gender is unclear (as might be the case with animal characters) make your best guess on the basis of factors such as clothing, vocal intonation, etc.

Role Behaviors: Indicate the number of male and female characters that engage in the role behaviors listed on the data sheet. Indicate the frequency with which male and female characters engage in these behaviors with a hatch mark.

Summarize your results and compare your findings to the research in your text by answering the questions that follow the coding sheet.

Children's Media Coding Sheet

Narrators	
Female Narrators:_____	Male Narrators:_____
Program Characters	
Male Characters:_____	Female Characters:_____

Roles	Male	Female
Aggressive		
Rescuing Others		
Submissive		
Passive		
Being Rescued		
Comic Roles		
Domestic Roles		
Positions of Authority		
Emotional		
Concerned with Physical Appearance		
Physically Fit		
Overweight		
Professional Occupation		
Service Occupation		
Other (Describe)		

1. Are males and females represented with equal frequency in children's media? Compare the frequency of female and male narrators and characters.

2. In what roles are females likely to be portrayed? What attributes do they share?

3. In what roles are males likely to be portrayed? What attributes do they share?

4.   What conclusions can you draw about gender stereotyping on television? Compare and contrast your findings to the research reported in your text.

5.   Based upon your observation, what suggestions would you have for parents concerned about exposing their children to gender stereotypes?

Adapted from Watson, David L. Portrayal of the sexes on TV. In Vivian P. Makosky et al. (Eds.), *Activities handbook for the teaching of psychology* (Vol. 3) (pp. 295–297). Washington, DC: American Psychological Association. Copyright © 1990 by the American Psychological Association. Adapted with permission.

PROJECT 5.6

CHILDREN'S TOYS: A CONTENT ANALYSIS OF TOY STORE MERCHANDISE

Purpose: This exercise is designed to explore the relationship of children's toys and play to the development of gender identity and the maintenance of gender roles.

Instructions: Take a trip to a local store that has a well-stocked toy department. You might select a specialty toy store or a discount department store that has a wide selection of toys for children of different ages. Spend about one hour examining the toys and packaging materials and making notes about the extent to which you observe evidence of gender stereotyping and gender-specific messages.

In your analysis consider colors (e.g., pastels, black, red), pictures of boys or girls on the packaging, and specific indications of gender (e.g., "for girls aged 4 to 6 years"). In addition, consider factors such as placement in the store (for example, are all of the dolls in the same aisle as the bake sets?) or the interest that young children in the store might express toward certain toys.

Summarize your results by responding to the questions that follow:

1. What were your first reactions? Are the toys different from those you recall from your childhood?

2.   Did you find that some toys were related to adult gender roles (for example, housewife, doctor, etc.)? Which ones?

3.   How would you characterize boys' toys? What were their most common attributes or uses? Compare and contrast your observation to the material in your text.

4. How would you characterize girls' toys? What were their most common attributes or uses? Compare and contrast your observation to the material in your text.

5. Did you find any toys that might be considered to be gender neutral? Which ones? What proportion of the toys would you estimate fell into this category?

Adapted from Lloyd, Margaret A. Gender-role stereotyping in toys: An out-of-class project. In Vivian P. Makosky et al. (Eds.), *Activities handbook for the teaching of psychology* (Vol. 3) (pp. 293–294). Washington, DC: American Psychological Association. Copyright © 1990 by the American Psychological Association. Adapted with permission.

CHAPTER 6

COGNITION, EDUCATION, AND ACHIEVEMENT

PROJECT 6.1

POPULAR CONCEPTIONS OF GENDER DIFFERENCES IN COGNITIVE ABILITIES: HOW ARE MEN AND WOMEN DIFFERENT?

Purpose: This exercise is another replication of Swim's (1994) investigation of people's perceptions of the sizes of gender differences compared with the results of meta-analytic studies.

Instructions: Recruit two women and two men who are willing to complete a short questionnaire that assesses popular conceptions of the gender differences in mental abilities that have been studied by psychologists. Select a variety of participants for this project. Include four people who vary not only by sex but by other social categories (for example, age, race or ethnicity, sexual orientation, social class, etc.). Be sure to describe each participant by indicating her or his sex, age, and social attributes (for example, race or ethnicity, social class, etc.) at the top of each interview form.

Explain to your volunteers that the questionnaire contains descriptions of five traits or behaviors. Your participants should read each description and think about whether they believe men and women differ on the attribute. Then, they should provide their estimation of the size of the gender difference using this scale.

-3: Women are more likely than men to have this ability. There is a large gender difference favoring women.

-2: Women are more likely than men to have this ability. There is a moderate gender difference favoring women.

-1: Women are more likely than men to have this ability. There is a small gender difference favoring women.

 0: No difference. Women and men are equally likely to have this ability.

+1: Men are more likely than women to have this ability. There is a small gender difference favoring men.

+2: Men are more likely than women to have this ability. There is a moderate gender difference favoring men.

+3: Men are more likely than women to have this ability. There is a large gender difference favoring men.

Participant A

Sex _____   Age _____

Characteristics/Comments_____

===

Psychologists have studied whether men and women differ on each of the following mental abilities. In some cases large gender differences have been found. In others, small to no gender differences have been established. Read each of the following descriptions and provide your estimate of the degree to which women and men (as a group) differ on each trait or behavior.

1. *Mathematics Ability:* Who receives higher scores on general mathematical achievement tests and problem-solving? Males or females?

    Estimation of gender difference: _____

2. *Scores on the Math SAT:* Who scores higher on the mathematics subscale of the SAT (Scholastic Aptitude Test)? Adolescent girls or boys?

    Estimation of gender difference: _____

3. *Verbal Tests:* Who receives higher scores on tests of verbal performance? This includes tests such as anagrams (scrambled letters that form words), vocabulary, reading comprehension, writing skills, etc. Males or females?

    Estimation of gender difference: _____

4. *Scores on the Verbal SAT:* Who scores higher on the verbal subscale of the SAT (Scholastic Aptitude Test)? Adolescent girls or boys?

    Estimation of gender difference: _____

5. *Scores on IQ Tests:* Who scores higher on measures of general intelligence? These are standardized tests such as the WAIS (Wechsler Adult Intelligence Scale). Males or females?

    Estimation of gender difference: _____

Participant B

Sex _____   Age _____

Characteristics/Comments_____

Psychologists have studied whether men and women differ on each of the following mental abilities. In some cases large gender differences have been found. In others, small to no gender differences have been established. Read each of the following descriptions and provide your estimate of the degree to which women and men (as a group) differ on each trait or behavior.

1. *Mathematics Ability:* Who receives higher scores on general mathematical achievement tests and problem-solving? Males or females?

   Estimation of gender difference: _____

2. *Scores on the Math SAT:* Who scores higher on the mathematics subscale of the SAT (Scholastic Aptitude Test)? Adolescent girls or boys?

   Estimation of gender difference: _____

3. *Verbal Tests:* Who receives higher scores on tests of verbal performance? This includes tests such as anagrams (scrambled letters that form words), vocabulary, reading comprehension, writing skills, etc. Males or females?

   Estimation of gender difference: _____

4. *Scores on the Verbal SAT:* Who scores higher on the verbal subscale of the SAT (Scholastic Aptitude Test)? Adolescent girls or boys?

   Estimation of gender difference: _____

5. *Scores on IQ Tests:* Who scores higher on measures of general intelligence? These are standardized tests such as the WAIS (Wechsler Adult Intelligence Scale). Males or females?

   Estimation of gender difference: _____

Participant C

Sex _____ Age _____

Characteristics/Comments_____

Psychologists have studied whether men and women differ on each of the following mental abilities. In some cases large gender differences have been found. In others, small to no gender differences have been established. Read each of the following descriptions and provide your estimate of the degree to which women and men (as a group) differ on each trait or behavior.

1. *Mathematics Ability:* Who receives higher scores on general mathematical achievement tests and problem-solving? Males or females?

   Estimation of gender difference: _____

2. *Scores on the Math SAT:* Who scores higher on the mathematics subscale of the SAT (Scholastic Aptitude Test)? Adolescent girls or boys?

   Estimation of gender difference: _____

3. *Verbal Tests:* Who receives higher scores on tests of verbal performance? This includes tests such as anagrams (scrambled letters that form words), vocabulary, reading comprehension, writing skills, etc. Males or females?

   Estimation of gender difference: _____

4. *Scores on the Verbal SAT:* Who scores higher on the verbal subscale of the SAT (Scholastic Aptitude Test)? Adolescent girls or boys?

   Estimation of gender difference: _____

5. *Scores on IQ Tests:* Who scores higher on measures of general intelligence? These are standardized tests such as the WAIS (Wechsler Adult Intelligence Scale). Males or females?

   Estimation of gender difference: _____

Participant D

Sex _____   Age _____

Characteristics/Comments_____

Psychologists have studied whether men and women differ on each of the following mental abilities. In some cases large gender differences have been found. In others, small to no gender differences have been established. Read each of the following descriptions and provide your estimate of the degree to which women and men (as a group) differ on each trait or behavior.

1. *Mathematics Ability:* Who receives higher scores on general mathematical achievement tests and problem-solving? Males or females?

    Estimation of gender difference: _____

2. *Scores on the Math SAT:* Who scores higher on the mathematics subscale of the SAT (Scholastic Aptitude Test)? Adolescent girls or boys?

    Estimation of gender difference: _____

3. *Verbal Tests:* Who receives higher scores on tests of verbal performance? This includes tests such as anagrams (scrambled letters that form words), vocabulary, reading comprehension, writing skills, etc. Males or females?

    Estimation of gender difference: _____

4. *Scores on the Verbal SAT:* Who scores higher on the verbal subscale of the SAT (Scholastic Aptitude Test)? Adolescent girls or boys?

    Estimation of gender difference: _____

5. *Scores on IQ Tests:* Who scores higher on measures of general intelligence? These are standardized tests such as the WAIS (Wechsler Adult Intelligence Scale). Males or females?

    Estimation of gender difference: _____

Summarize your results by answering the questions below.

1.   Swim found that her college-student samples generally provided accurate estimations or underestimated gender differences. What were your findings?

2.   One difference that was consistently overestimated in Swim's study was the gender difference in verbal abilities (that is, women's verbal abilities were overestimated). Did you find similar results?

3. One difference that was consistently underestimated in Swim's study was the gender difference in mathematical abilities. Did you find similar results? Do you find this surprising considering the material in your text about attitudes about mathematics?

4. Swim suggested that the high level of accuracy exhibited in her sample might be due to the fact that it was composed of college students (aged 18 to 22) who might be likely to underestimate gender differences. Comment on this possibility, especially if your participants were not traditional college students.

Reference: Swim, Janet K. (1994). Perceived versus meta-analytic effect sizes: An assessment of the accuracy of gender stereotypes. *Journal of Personality and Social Psychology, 66,* 21–36.

PROJECT 6.2

MATHEMATICS, SCIENCE, AND GENDER: AN AUTOBIOGRAPHICAL PROJECT

Purpose: This exercise is designed for you to explore the social and affective variables that are related to gender differences in achievement in mathematics and science.

Instructions: Like most gender differences, socialization interacts with biological factors to contribute to the different experiences of women and men. In this project you will write an autobiography about your academic experiences in mathematics and science.

1. What sort of training have you had in mathematics and science? How many math courses have you taken? How many science courses have you taken? Which ones?

   Math:

   Science:

2. Did you participate in any extracurricular activities involving these subjects? For example, were you a member of the science club in high school or did you participate in science fairs?

3.	What sort of messages did you get about boys' and girls' abilities in math and science while you were growing up? Consider the following sources:

Parents:

Peers/Siblings:

Teachers:

4.	There are significant differences between racial/ethnic groups in achievement in math and science. Do you feel that your family's cultural background influenced your attitudes toward math and science? How?

5.	In general, how well have you done in math classes? Science classes?

6. What are your career goals? Do you expect to hold a job that requires a lot of knowledge and skill in math and science? Why or why not?

7. Describe two of your most memorable experiences with math or science. One experience should be positive and one experience should be negative.

    Positive:

    Negative:

8. Relate these perceptions and experiences to the text's discussion of the relationship of socialization to gender differences in achievement. How are your experiences similar to patterns found in the research? How are your experiences different?

PROJECT 6.3

GENDER AND COMPUTERS: WHO USES COMPUTERS, AND HOW DO THEY FEEL ABOUT THEM?

Purpose: This project is designed to have you investigate differences and similarities in women's and men's attitudes toward computers and their use.

Instructions: Researchers are just beginning to study gender differences and similarities in computer use. For example, although estimates vary tremendously, it is thought that the majority of users on the Internet are men. Other researchers have begun to find gender differences in experience with computers and computer games. As gender-role socialization is related to gender differences in attitudes and achievement in math and the sciences, it is possible that it also will be related to gender differences in computer literacy.

Drop in at the campus computer center and conduct an observational study of the environment. After you have summarized the setting by completing the Environment Coding Sheet, interview two men and two women about their experiences with computers. Try to recruit volunteers who differ on social variables such as race or ethnicity. Record their answers on the four data sheets provided for this use.

Be courteous, and do not interrupt people in their work. A good strategy would be to stand outside the main entrance and ask people to volunteer as they are leaving the computer center.

After you have completed the data sheets, summarize your results by answering the questions at the end of this project. Refer to your data from your observational study and your interviews.

Environment Coding Sheet

Briefly describe the environment of the computer center by answering these questions:

1. How many men are using computers in the center? How many women?

2. How many of the support staff are men? How many are women?

3. Count the number of women and men engaged in the following activities:

	Women	Men
Word processing	_____	_____
Sending/reading e-mail	_____	_____
Surfing the Web	_____	_____
Programming	_____	_____
Playing games	_____	_____

4. Include any other observations that you find relevant.

Participant A

Sex _____   Age   _____

Characteristics/Comments_____

1.   Please tell me the different uses you have for computers. Examples: word
     processing, e-mail, access to the World Wide Web, programming,
     statistics, etc.

2.   Do you play video or computer games? If so, which ones? How often?
     About how many hours per week?

3.   Are you planning on going into a career that will require you to use
     computers? If so, what computer skills will you need to have?

4.   How comfortable do you feel using computers? Would you say that you're
     computer literate? Why or why not?

Participant B

Sex _____   Age _____

Characteristics/Comments_____

1. Please tell me the different uses you have for computers. Examples: word
    processing, e-mail, access to the World Wide Web, programming,
    statistics, etc.

2. Do you play video or computer games? If so, which ones? How often?
    About how many hours per week?

3. Are you planning on going into a career that will require you to use
    computers? If so, what computer skills will you need to have?

4. How comfortable do you feel using computers? Would you say that you're
    computer literate? Why or why not?

Participant C

Sex _____   Age _____

Characteristics/Comments_____

1. Please tell me the different uses you have for computers. Examples: word processing, e-mail, access to the World Wide Web, programming, statistics, etc.

2. Do you play video or computer games? If so, which ones? How often? About how many hours per week?

3. Are you planning on going into a career that will require you to use computers? If so, what computer skills will you need to have?

4. How comfortable do you feel using computers? Would you say that you're computer literate? Why or why not?

Participant D

Sex _____   Age   _____

Characteristics/Comments_____

1.   Please tell me the different uses you have for computers. Examples: word processing, e-mail, access to the World Wide Web, programming, statistics, etc.

2.   Do you play video or computer games? If so, which ones? How often? About how many hours per week?

3.   Are you planning on going into a career that will require you to use computers? If so, what computer skills will you need to have?

4.   How comfortable do you feel using computers? Would you say that you're computer literate? Why or why not?

1. Do women and men use computers differently, or would you say there are no gender differences in the use of computers?

2. Are there gender differences and similarities in the use of computer or video games? Do men and women choose the same games? Do they play games with equal frequency?

3. Compare and contrast women's and men's attitudes toward computers.

4. Did you find gender differences or similarities in attitudes toward computers and computer literacy? Describe your findings.

5. Can you relate your results to the research on attitudes and achievement in math and science? What implications might different experiences with computers have on men's and women's achievement?

PROJECT 6.4

WHO INSPIRED YOU? MENTORS AND ROLE MODELS

Purpose: The purpose of this exercise is to have you consider the ways in which role models influenced your attitudes toward academic and vocational achievement.

Instructions: Think about a person you knew personally who you saw as a model of achievement. This might be a parent or relative, a teacher or employer, a neighbor, a friend, etc. Consider how this person influenced your attitudes toward school and work.

1. Describe this person. What attributes or qualities made this person a mentor or role model?

2. What messages did this person give you about your academic abilities?

3. Did you receive different messages about academic failures and successes? If so, what were they?

4. How did this person influence your choice of career, either present or future?

5. Consider the research in your text on the influence of role models on academic achievement. Why do you think this person was so influential?

PROJECT 6.5

THE CLASSROOM CLIMATE AND ACADEMIC PERFORMANCE

Purpose: This exercise is designed to demonstrate the effects of a chilly classroom climate on academic attitudes and performance.

Instructions: Researchers investigating gender and racial/ethnic differences in achievement have focused on the classroom climate. The classroom climate might be considered to be warm and supportive for some students, the lucky ones who blossom, or chilly and hostile for others who are less lucky.

The gender and racial/ethnic stereotypes held by teachers can contribute to the classroom climate. As your text notes, teachers treat boys and girls (and also college women and men) in different ways. Often these gender differences interact with differential treatment based upon race or ethnicity. The result of this differential treatment is group differences in self-confidence and expectations for success in the course material.

Think about a situation in which you experienced a chilly classroom climate. Evaluate this experience by answering the following questions.

1. Describe the class and the classroom interaction. Do not identify the school or the instructor.

2. Did the instructor make different attributions about students' work? Which students succeeded because of luck? Effort? Ability? Did the instructor make different attributions for failure? If so, how?

3. Which students were called on the most? Which students received more time or attention? Why do you think they were picked?

4. Did the instructor make overgeneralizations about particular social groups (for example, Asians, women, gay men or lesbians, etc.)?

5. Were "jokes" made at the expense of others? This might include sexist, racist, or heterosexist remarks.

6. How did this climate affect you? How did you feel about your abilities? How did it affect your motivation?

Adapted from *Exploring/Teaching the Psychology of Women* (2nd ed.) by Michele A. Paludi by permission of the State University of New York Press. © 1996 State University of New York.

CHAPTER 7

GENDER AND THE WORKPLACE

PROJECT 7.1

OCCUPATIONAL SEGREGATION IN THE WORKPLACE

Purpose: This exercise is designed for you to assess the extent of occupational segregation as a function of sex and race in a specific work setting.

Instructions: Occupational segregation may be revealed in two ways. First, *segregation* occurs when the proportion of women and men in an occupational category is unequal. This might involve employment patterns such as a predominance of women in service occupations and/or a lack of ethnic minority workers in upper management. In this case, the majority of jobs are held by members of one group. Second, *stratification* occurs when the proportion of men and women might be equal within job categories but the women or men are clustered at certain occupational levels or tasks. A common example is the high concentration of female elementary school teachers and male principals or administrators. Labor force analyses indicate that occupational segregation is becoming less common among some occupations. On the other hand, the gender and racial composition of many occupational categories reflects patterns of inequality and segregation.

Conduct a survey of the employees on your campus. Using the occupational categories described below, complete the data sheet that follows and observe and summarize the gender and racial and ethnic composition of the campus work environments (that is, the administrative offices, food service, grounds crew, etc.). If you are enrolled at a very large campus, select representative departments for your survey. Hint: the telephone directory and university catalog also can be useful sources of information to supplement direct observation. Then, summarize your findings by answering the questions that follow the data sheet.

Professional / Managerial: This category includes professions such as accountants, engineers, physicians, scientists, and executives. These jobs require formal education and on-the-job experience. Typically, individuals in such positions have a significant level of responsibility and authority.

Blue Collar / Craft: These jobs are often considered trades and require a significant amount of on-the-job training or an apprenticeship. Examples are construction workers, plumbers, and heavy equipment drivers.

Clerical: This category includes jobs such as file clerk, secretary, data entry, bookkeeper operator, etc. Usually, some sort of on-the-job experience is required but the level of formal education demanded by the position may vary.

Service: These jobs are relatively low skilled and require a high level of contact with the public. Examples are cashier, sales clerk, and food server.

Occupational Segregation Data Sheet

Briefly describe the occupational patterns you have observed by answering these questions:

1. Approximately what proportion of men and women did you observe in each of the following categories?

	Men	Women
Professional/Managerial		
Blue Collar/Craft		
Clerical		
Service		

2. Among these categories, what proportion of the supervisors were men? What proportion were women?

	Men	Women
Blue Collar/Craft		
Clerical		
Service		

3. What is the composition of the faculty?

	Men	Women
Full Professor		
Associate Professor		
Assistant Professor		
Lecturer or Instructor		
Part-time or Adjunct		

4. Can you comment on the racial composition of each category? Do racial/ethnic minorities appear more frequently in one or more categories?

5. Consider the professional/managerial category. Did you find evidence for gender differences in this category? For example, were women managers more commonly found in traditionally female-dominated fields such as human resources and clerical services? Were male executives more likely to be found in departments such as finance?

6. Did you observe sex stratification among the faculty positions?

7.   Compare and contrast your findings to the material in the text. What conclusions can you make about the gender composition of the workplace?

7.   How are gender and race related? Are the experiences of women from minority groups different from those of European-American women? Men from minority groups? European-American men? How?

PROJECT 7.2

WOMEN AND MEN WORKING IN NONTRADITIONAL OCCUPATIONS

Purpose: This project is designed to consider the experiences of people who are working in occupations other than those that are typical for their gender.

Instructions: Much of the research on workers employed in nontraditional occupations (that is, women who work in male-dominated jobs and men who work in female-dominated jobs) has focused on one group, women in managerial or professional occupations. Less is known about the experience of women and men in other nontraditional occupations.

Using the interview schedule at the end of this exercise, interview a man or a woman who is working in a nontraditional job. Be creative, and try to interview someone other than a professional woman. You might want to interview a woman who is in a blue collar job (for example, a carpenter or truck driver) or a man who works in a female-dominated profession such as nursing or child care. Summarize your findings by answering the following questions.

1. Relate your findings to the text's discussion of the benefits and strains of women's and men's occupational roles. How are your findings representative of the research reported in the text?

2. How do your findings differ? To what factors do you attribute these differences? Consider such factors as support from family members, a flexible work environment, etc.

3. Did you find any evidence of gender discrimination in hiring, wages, or promotion (a glass ceiling)? Did you find any evidence of gender working to one's advantage in hiring, wages, or promotion (a glass escalator)?

4. Did your participant report any evidence of discrimination? If so, in what form?

Employment Interview Schedule

Sex _____   Age_____

Family Status_____

Characteristics/Comments_____

1.   What is your current occupation? What do you do? Where do you work? Are you in a union?

2.   How or why did you choose this occupation?

3.   What factors did you consider before you accepted this job?

4.   What are the best things about this job? What are the drawbacks?

5.   How do people react when they find out what you do?

6.   Do you think being a woman/man in this job is a benefit or a liability? Why or why not?

7.   Suppose another man/woman was interviewing for this position. What advice would you give him/her?

PROJECT 7.3

COMBINING WORK AND FAMILY: THE FAMILY AND MEDICAL LEAVE ACT

Purpose: This exercise is designed to test your knowledge of the Family and Medical Leave Act.

Instructions: The Family and Medical Leave Act (FMLA) was enacted in August 1993 and amended in April 1997. This legislation guarantees certain rights to employees who need to take time off from their jobs for personal or family reasons.

Do you know your rights under the FMLA? Take the self-quiz at the end of this exercise. After you have scored it, respond to the questions below.

1. How did you score?

What misconceptions did you have?

About which facts were you the most knowledgeable?

2. Consider the provisions of the FMLA according to the needs of employed family members facing personal and medical crises at home. In what ways might the FMLA be improved to better meet workers' needs? What changes could be made to encourage employees to take advantage of this benefit?

3. This self-quiz was based upon the FMLA at the time of this writing (spring 1997). Research the current status of the FMLA. Has additional legislation been passed? If so, how has it been changed?

The Family and Medical Leave Act

Self-Quiz

T   F   1. The FMLA guarantees workers up to 6 weeks of paid leave per year.

T   F   2. The FMLA covers leaves to care for all family members, including unmarried domestic partners.

T   F   3. All private, state, local, and federal employees are covered.

T   F   4. Employees may take their leave intermittently; they do not have to take their leave in a single block of time.

T   F   5. Health insurance benefits continue for the duration of covered leaves.

T   F   6. The FMLA covers instances when the employee is seriously ill.

T   F   7. Whereas serious health conditions are covered, mental health disorders are not.

T   F   8. Eligible employees may take FMLA leave following the adoption of a child or placement of a foster child.

T   F   9. Employees who are designated as "key workers" (salaried employees who are among the highest paid 10%) are not covered under the FMLA.

T   F   10. The FMLA guarantees employees their original or equivalent job upon their return.

T   F   11. Federal employees are eligible for up to 24 hours of unpaid leave per year for family matters and emergencies.

T   F   12. Spouses who work for the same employer may take a combined total of 24 weeks of family leave.

T   F   13. Chronic and long-term conditions (such as asthma, cancer, diabetes, or Alzheimer's) are covered.

T   F   14. Employees may not use accrued sick or vacation leave to cover some of their leave under the FMLA.

The answers to these questions appear on the following page.

The Family and Medical Leave Act

Scoring Key

1. *False*. Workers are guaranteed 12 weeks of unpaid leave per year.

2. *False*. The FMLA provides for leaves to care for immediate family members only (defined as spouses, children, or parents).

3. *False*. All public agencies and local education agencies are covered in addition to private sector employers with fifty or more employees within a 75-mile area.

4. *True*. The FMLA allows employees to take intermittent leave over blocks of time or by reducing their normal work schedule.

5. *True*. Group health insurance coverage is maintained for all covered employees.

6. *True*. Employees who experience serious health conditions are covered under the FMLA.

7. *False*. Physical or mental conditions are covered.

8. *True*. The FMLA applies to placement for adoption and foster care as well as childbirth.

9. *True*. Key workers are exempt.

10. *True*. Employees are guaranteed restoration of their original job, or an equivalent (in terms of pay, benefits, and conditions of employment).

11. *True*. Benefits for federal workers were expanded in April 1993.

12. *False*. Covered spouses who work for the same employer are restricted to a combined total of 12 weeks leave.

13. *True*. Acute, chronic, or long-term conditions are covered.

14. *False*. In certain cases, employees' paid leave may count as FMLA leave.

References: *Employment Standards Administration Wage and Hour Division. Fact Sheet No. 028. The Family and Medical Leave Act of 1993* [Online]. Available URL: www.dol.gov/dol/esa/public/regs/cfr/fmla/825-001.htm

Jackson, Robert L. (1997, April 13). Clinton expands unpaid leave for federal workers. *The Los Angeles Times*, pp. A1, A22.

PROJECT 7.4

THE SEXIST EMPLOYMENT INTERVIEWERS

Purpose: This exercise is designed to develop your understanding of the roles sexism can play in job discrimination and pay equity for both men and women.

Instructions: Before the passage of the Equal Pay Act of 1963 and the Civil Rights Act of 1964 (and as amended by the Equal Employment Opportunity Act of 1972) employers could (and did) place separate advertisements for positions, listing positions such as "Girl Friday" or placing ads under separate "Help Wanted—Male" and "Help Wanted—Female" sections in the classifieds. Since the passage of this legislation, employers cannot legally ask questions about a number of variables. These include biological sex (males and females are protected), racial or ethnic background, sexual orientation, marital status, and "pregnancy, childbirth or related conditions."

Access discrimination (or sex discrimination at the time of hiring) still may occur, however, in the form of subtly sexist questions. For example, marital status might be probed by asking the seemingly trivial question "Which form of address do you prefer, Mrs. or Miss?" This question, under the current legislation, is illegal. Questions regarding sex, sexual orientation, marital status, and pregnancy are legal only in cases where these variables are a bona fide occupational qualification (BFOQ) of the job category that is necessary for the normal operation of the business. In these instances, the employer must demonstrate that members of the excluded group cannot perform the *essential* duties of the job that are reasonably necessary for the normal operation of business. For example, whereas a restaurant might *prefer* to hire women servers, in this case sex is not a BFOQ for the job (that is, women and men can effectively wait tables).

Read the following scenarios that depict a woman and a man in an employment interview. Then, keeping these guidelines in mind, respond to the questions that follow each.

Reference: Player, Mack A. (1992). *Federal law of employment discrimination* (3rd ed.). St. Paul, MN: West.

Julia Hernandez is a single woman who is applying for a management trainee position in a local firm. She will receive her bachelor's degree in business and management in less than two weeks. Her training fits the job requirements, and she maintained a 3.5 GPA in college.

John Washington, Director of Human Resources, is looking over her job application prior to the interview. He notes her academic record, strong letters of recommendation, and overall qualifications. On the other hand, he really wonders whether she would be right for the position. The company puts a lot of money into its management training program and has a significant investment in each trainee. What if she winds up getting married or pregnant and quits? Wouldn't it be better to have a man in this position?

1. What questions can John *legally* ask Julia that address his concerns?

2. What *illegal* questions might John ask Julia?

3. How do you think Julia should respond to these questions and convince John that she's the best candidate for this position?

Elliot Lee, an attractive single man, is applying for a position as receptionist/secretary to the executive vice president of outside sales. One critical requirement for the position is good people skills because there is a lot of contact with sales representatives and clients. Elliot has excellent computer and word processing skills and graduated with honors after working his way through business school as a fashion model.

Jane Stone has interviewed Elliot, but thinks that a man wouldn't make a good secretary. After all, he is probably only looking at this job as a stop-gap until he can find a better position. In fact, she thinks that the amount of public contact will be a problem. What sort of man would want to work as a receptionist/secretary—won't the people he's dealing with think that he's gay?

1. What questions can Jane *legally* ask Elliot that address her concerns?

2. What *illegal* questions might Jane ask Elliot?

3. How do you think Elliot should respond to these questions and convince Jane that he's the best candidate for this position?

Jan Wong, an Asian American woman, has passed the written examination that is one of the hurdles before being accepted as an officer trainee with the police department in her home town. Jan was a varsity athlete in high school, has volunteered for a number of community services, and has been active in the local chapter of Girl Scouts since her graduation from the police academy.

The members of the interview panel are concerned about Jan's application. She did pass the physical health exam and is within the parameters of the physical requirements for admission to the academy. On the other hand, how effective will she be when it comes to apprehending criminals (especially if they're men)? Would Jan be accepted as an equal by the predominantly male police force? Jan barely meets the physical requirements—will she be able to withstand the rigors of the job? Will the public take her seriously?

1. What questions can the interviewers *legally* ask Jan that address these concerns?

2. What *illegal* questions might they ask Jan?

3. How do you think Jan should respond to these questions and convince the interviewers that she's a good candidate for admission?

PROJECT 7.5

SEXUAL HARASSMENT ON THE COLLEGE CAMPUS

Purpose: This exercise involves researching the policy regarding sexual harassment on your campus.

Instructions: Obtain a copy of the policy regarding sexual harassment on your campus. Compare this policy with the description of the Equal Employment Opportunity Commission's guidelines given in your text. Then answer the following questions.

1.   Who is covered by this policy? Faculty? Students? Administrators? Staff?

2.   How is quid pro quo harassment (i.e., unwanted sexual advances as a condition of employment, promotion, etc.) identified? Are any examples provided?

3.   How is a hostile work environment identified and addressed? List any examples.

4. How is gender-based harassment (behaviors that are not explicitly sexual) identified and addressed?

5. What are the procedures for filing a complaint?

6. How are complaints handled? Which campus organizations, departments, and/or staff members are responsible for adjudicating complaints?

7. What are the statistics for your campus? How many women report cases of harassment? How many men?

CHAPTER 8

SEXUALITY

PROJECT 8.1

FEMALE AND MALE SEXUAL AND REPRODUCTIVE ANATOMY

Purpose: This exercise is designed to provide a review and self-test of reproductive anatomy and physiology.

Instructions: This exercise will be most helpful if you complete it after becoming familiar with the text and lecture material on reproductive anatomy. Without looking at the text and/or lecture notes, turn to the following four pages and draw the male and female reproductive organs. Each page contains a list of internal and external organs that should be represented in each drawing.

After you have completed your drawings, compare them with your text and lecture materials. Using a different color pen and pencil, correct any inaccuracies and add any organs you were unable to draw from memory.

Review your errors and omissions. As an added review, can you describe the function of each structure?

Internal Female Anatomy

Include the following structures:

Vagina   Grafenberg spot (G-spot)

Cervix   Ovaries

Uterus   Bladder

Fallopian tubes   Urethra

Internal Male Anatomy

Include the following structures:

Testes   Urethra

Vas deferens   Bladder

Prostate   Cowper's gland

Seminal glands

External Female Anatomy

Include the following structures:

Vaginal opening   Clitoris

Labia majora   Clitoral hood

Labia minora   Urethral opening

External Male Anatomy

Include the following structures:

Penis   Urethral opening

Scrotum   Foreskin

Glans penis

PROJECT 8.2

POPULAR CONCEPTIONS OF GENDER DIFFERENCES IN SEXUAL BEHAVIOR AND ATTITUDES: HOW ARE MEN AND WOMEN DIFFERENT?

Purpose: This exercise is designed to assess people's beliefs about gender differences and similarities in sexual behavior and attitudes and compare them to Oliver and Hyde's (1993) meta-analysis of a large number of surveys.

Instructions: Recruit two women and two men who are willing to complete a short questionnaire that assesses popular conceptions of the gender differences that have been studied by psychologists. Include four people who vary not only by sex but by other social categories (for example, age, race or ethnicity, sexual orientation, social class, etc.). Be sure to describe each participant by indicating her or his sex, age, and social attributes (for example, race or ethnicity, social class, etc.) at the top of each interview form.

Explain to your volunteers that the questionnaire contains descriptions of sexual attitudes or behaviors. Your participants should read each description and think about whether they believe men and women differ on the trait or behavior. Then, they should provide their estimation of the size of this gender difference using this scale.

-3: Women are more likely than men to have permissive attitudes or engage in this behavior. There is a large gender difference favoring women.

-2: Women are more likely than men to have permissive attitudes or engage in this behavior. There is a moderate gender difference favoring women.

-1: Women are more likely than men to have permissive attitudes or engage in this behavior. There is a small gender difference favoring women.

0: No difference. Women's and men's attitudes or behaviors are similar.

+1: Men are more likely than women to have permissive attitudes or engage in this behavior. There is a small gender difference favoring men.

+2: Men are more likely than women to have permissive attitudes or engage in this behavior. There is a moderate gender difference favoring men.

+3: Men are more likely than women to have permissive attitudes or engage in this behavior. There is a large gender difference favoring men.

Participant A

Sex _____   Age _____

Characteristics/Comments_____

Psychologists have studied whether men and women differ on each of the following behaviors or traits. In some cases large gender differences have been found. In others, small to no gender differences have been established. Read each of the following descriptions and provide your estimate of the degree to which women and men (as a group) differ on each trait or behavior.

1. *Seuxal Permissiveness:* In general, do men or women hold more permissive attitudes toward sex?

    Estimation of gender difference: _____

2. *Double Standard:* Who is more likely to advocate the double standard (that is, premarital sex is acceptable for men, but not women)? Men or women?

    Estimation of gender difference: _____

3. *Masturbation:* Who is more likely to masturbate? Men or women?

    Estimation of gender difference: _____

4. *Frequency of Intercourse:* Do women or men report having intercourse more frequently?

    Estimation of gender difference: _____

5. *Number of Sexual Partners:* Who reports a larger number of sexual partners in a lifetime? Women or men?

    Estimation of gender difference: _____

6. *Attitudes Toward Homosexuality:* Do women or men report more permissive attitudes toward homosexuality?

    Estimation of gender difference: _____

Participant B

Sex _____   Age _____

Characteristics/Comments_____

Psychologists have studied whether men and women differ on each of the following behaviors or traits. In some cases large gender differences have been found. In others, small to no gender differences have been established. Read each of the following descriptions and provide your estimate of the degree to which women and men (as a group) differ on each trait or behavior.

1. *Seuxal Permissiveness:* In general, do men or women hold more permissive attitudes toward sex?

    Estimation of gender difference: _____

2. *Double Standard:* Who is more likely to advocate the double standard (that is, premarital sex is acceptable for men, but not women)? Men or women?

    Estimation of gender difference: _____

3. *Masturbation:* Who is more likely to masturbate? Men or women?

    Estimation of gender difference: _____

4. *Frequency of Intercourse*: Do women or men report having intercourse more frequently?

    Estimation of gender difference: _____

5. *Number of Sexual Partners:* Who reports a larger number of sexual partners in a lifetime? Women or men?

    Estimation of gender difference: _____

6. *Attitudes Toward Homosexuality:* Do women or men report more permissive attitudes toward homosexuality?

    Estimation of gender difference: _____

Participant C

Sex _____   Age _____

Characteristics/Comments_____

Psychologists have studied whether men and women differ on each of the following behaviors or traits. In some cases large gender differences have been found. In others, small to no gender differences have been established. Read each of the following descriptions and provide your estimate of the degree to which women and men (as a group) differ on each trait or behavior.

1. *Seuxal Permissiveness:* In general, do men or women hold more permissive attitudes toward sex?

    Estimation of gender difference: _____

2. *Double Standard:* Who is more likely to advocate the double standard (that is, premarital sex is acceptable for men, but not women)? Men or women?

    Estimation of gender difference: _____

3. *Masturbation:* Who is more likely to masturbate? Men or women?

    Estimation of gender difference: _____

4. *Frequency of Intercourse*: Do women or men report having intercourse more frequently?

    Estimation of gender difference: _____

5. *Number of Sexual Partners:* Who reports a larger number of sexual partners in a lifetime? Women or men?

    Estimation of gender difference: _____

6. *Attitudes Toward Homosexuality:* Do women or men report more permissive attitudes toward homosexuality?

    Estimation of gender difference: _____

Participant D

Sex _____   Age   _____

Characteristics/Comments_____

Psychologists have studied whether men and women differ on each of the following behaviors or traits. In some cases large gender differences have been found. In others, small to no gender differences have been established. Read each of the following descriptions and provide your estimate of the degree to which women and men (as a group) differ on each trait or behavior.

1. *Seuxal Permissiveness:* In general, do men or women hold more permissive attitudes toward sex?

    Estimation of gender difference: _____

2. *Double Standard:* Who is more likely to advocate the double standard (that is, premarital sex is acceptable for men, but not women)? Men or women?

    Estimation of gender difference: _____

3. *Masturbation:* Who is more likely to masturbate? Men or women?

    Estimation of gender difference: _____

4. *Frequency of Intercourse*: Do women or men report having intercourse more frequently?

    Estimation of gender difference: _____

5. *Number of Sexual Partners:* Who reports a larger number of sexual partners in a lifetime? Women or men?

    Estimation of gender difference: _____

6. *Attitudes Toward Homosexuality:* Do women or men report more permissive attitudes toward homosexuality?

    Estimation of gender difference: _____

Summarize your results by answering the questions below.

1. Oliver and Hyde (1993) report large gender differences favoring men on these variables. How accurate were your respondents?

Sexual permissiveness

Masturbation

Frequency of intercourse

Number of sexual partners

2. Were your respondents accurate in estimating the small difference favoring men in the number of sexual partners reported? Did your respondents accurately estimate no gender differences in attitudes toward homosexuality?

3. Evaluate your respondents' knowledge of these gender differences and similarities. Some of the findings from this meta-analysis are consistent with gender stereotypes and sexual scripts whereas other findings are contradictory. Were your respondents more likely to estimate differences along the lines of traditional stereotypes? Or were your respondents more likely to underestimate differences?

Reference: Oliver, Mary B., & Hyde, Janet S. (1993). Gender differences in sexuality: A meta-analysis. *Psychological Bulletin, 114*, 29–51.

PROJECT 8.3

EVALUATING METHODS OF CONTRACEPTION

Purpose: This exercise requires you to research and evaluate two methods of birth control.

Instructions: Pick one method of birth control from each of the lists below. One method should be a non-prescription (over-the-counter) method and the other should be available by prescription only. After you have chosen your methods, complete the evaluation worksheets that follow. Over-the-counter methods may be researched by visiting a local pharmacy, although you might wish to obtain further information from the campus library and health center. Prescription methods may be researched by visiting the campus health center or a local clinic. You also might wish to supplement your visit with some research at the campus library.

Non-prescription Methods	Prescription Methods
Male Condom	Oral Contraceptives (the Pill)
Female Condom	Depo Provera
Spermicide—Foam	Norplant
Spermicide—Vaginal Film	IUD
Spermicide and Condom	Diaphragm
Natural Family Planning/Fertility Awareness	Cervical Cap

Contraceptive Evaluation Sheet

1. What method did you choose? Is it available over the counter or by prescription? How much does it cost?

2. How does this method work?

3. What is the failure rate?

4. How long is this method effective?

5. What are two advantages of this method?

6. What are two disadvantages of this method?

7. Does this method provide protection against sexually transmitted diseases (STDs)?

Contraceptive Evaluation Sheet

1. What method did you choose? Is it available over the counter or by prescription? How much does it cost?

2. How does this method work?

3. What is the failure rate?

4. How long is this method effective?

5. What are two advantages of this method?

6. What are two disadvantages of this method?

7. Does this method provide protection against sexually transmitted diseases (STDs)?

PROJECT 8.4

INFLUENCING A PARTNER TO USE A CONDOM

Purpose: This project is a replication of DeBro and colleagues' research investigating heterosexual college students' strategies for encouraging a partner to agree to use a condom.

Instructions: Recruit two women and two men who are willing to complete a short questionnaire that assesses how comfortable they would feel discussing the use of a condom with a potential sex partner. Include four people who vary not only by sex but by other social categories (for example, age, race or ethnicity, social class, etc.).

Explain to your volunteers that the questionnaire contains descriptions of strategies people might engage in to encourage a partner to use a condom. Make sure that they understand that their responses are anonymous. Due to the sensitive nature of this material, it would be best to ensure that your respondents return their questionnaires to you in a sealed envelope.

After the four worksheets have been returned to you, summarize your data by responding to these questions:

1. DeBro and her colleagues found that college students stereotyped the use of influence strategies along gender lines. They believed that women were more likely to use strategies to *encourage* condom use whereas men were more likely to use strategies to *avoid* condom use. What were your findings?

2. These researchers found that men reported higher comfort and effectiveness ratings for the use of seduction than did women. In contrast, women's comfort and effectiveness ratings were higher than men's for providing risk information or withholding sex. What were your findings?

3. Evaluate your results by considering the nature of heterosexual sexual scripts. How do these results relate to the double standard of sexual behavior for heterosexual women and men?

Reference: DeBro, Sherrine C., Campbell, Susan M., & Peplau, Letitia A. (1994). Influencing a partner to use a condom: A college student perspective. *Psychology of Women Quarterly, 18,* 165–182.

Participant A

Sex _____   Age _____

People may try a number of strategies to persuade a potential sex partner to use a condom in order to provide protection against sexually transmitted diseases (STDs). Read each of the six strategies below. Then indicate how effective you think the strategy would be and how comfortable you would feel using each strategy.

1.   Promising a reward (for example, how happy you would be, or how the relationship would be improved).

   1   2   3   4   5   6   7
Very ineffective   Very effective

   1   2   3   4   5   6   7
Very uncomfortable   Very comfortable

2.   Using emotional threats (for example, how angry and hurt you would be).

   1   2   3   4   5   6   7
Very ineffective   Very effective

   1   2   3   4   5   6   7
Very uncomfortable   Very comfortable

3.   Providing information about the health risks of STDs.

   1   2   3   4   5   6   7
Very ineffective   Very effective

   1   2   3   4   5   6   7
Very uncomfortable   Very comfortable

4.   Using deception or making up a different reason (like fear of pregnancy).

   1   2   3   4   5   6   7
Very ineffective   Very effective

   1   2   3   4   5   6   7
Very uncomfortable   Very comfortable

5.   Using seduction (for example, getting your partner aroused, putting on the condom as a part of sex play).

<table>
<tr><td>1</td><td>2</td><td>3</td><td>4</td><td>5</td><td>6</td><td>7</td></tr>
</table>

Very ineffective   Very effective

<table>
<tr><td>1</td><td>2</td><td>3</td><td>4</td><td>5</td><td>6</td><td>7</td></tr>
</table>

Very uncomfortable   Very comfortable

6.   Withholding sex (saying "no condom, no sex").

<table>
<tr><td>1</td><td>2</td><td>3</td><td>4</td><td>5</td><td>6</td><td>7</td></tr>
</table>

Very ineffective   Very effective

<table>
<tr><td>1</td><td>2</td><td>3</td><td>4</td><td>5</td><td>6</td><td>7</td></tr>
</table>

Very uncomfortable   Very comfortable

The last two questions concern your beliefs about heterosexual men and women's attitudes toward condoms.

7.   Who do you think is more likely to encourage the use of a condom? (circle one):

   Men   Women   Both equally likely

8.   Who do you think is more likely to avoid using a condom? (circle one):

   Men   Women   Both equally likely

Participant B

Sex _____   Age _____

People may try a number of strategies to persuade a potential sex partner to use a condom in order to provide protection against sexually transmitted diseases (STDs). Read each of the six strategies below. Then indicate how effective you think the strategy would be and how comfortable you would feel using each strategy.

1.   Promising a reward (for example, how happy you would be, or how the relationship would be improved).

       1   2   3   4   5   6   7
Very ineffective   Very effective

       1   2   3   4   5   6   7
Very uncomfortable   Very comfortable

2.   Using emotional threats (for example, how angry and hurt you would be).

       1   2   3   4   5   6   7
Very ineffective   Very effective

       1   2   3   4   5   6   7
Very uncomfortable   Very comfortable

3.   Providing information about the health risks of STDs.

       1   2   3   4   5   6   7
Very ineffective   Very effective

       1   2   3   4   5   6   7
Very uncomfortable   Very comfortable

4.   Using deception or making up a different reason (like fear of pregnancy).

       1   2   3   4   5   6   7
Very ineffective   Very effective

       1   2   3   4   5   6   7
Very uncomfortable   Very comfortable

5. Using seduction (for example, getting your partner aroused, putting on the condom as a part of sex play).

| 1 | 2 | 3 | 4 | 5 | 6 | 7 |
| Very ineffective | | | | | | Very effective |

| 1 | 2 | 3 | 4 | 5 | 6 | 7 |
| Very uncomfortable | | | | | | Very comfortable |

6. Withholding sex (saying "no condom, no sex").

| 1 | 2 | 3 | 4 | 5 | 6 | 7 |
| Very ineffective | | | | | | Very effective |

| 1 | 2 | 3 | 4 | 5 | 6 | 7 |
| Very uncomfortable | | | | | | Very comfortable |

The last two questions concern your beliefs about heterosexual men and women's attitudes toward condoms.

7. Who do you think is more likely to encourage the use of a condom? (circle one):

Men   Women   Both equally likely

8. Who do you think is more likely to avoid using a condom? (circle one):

Men   Women   Both equally likely

Participant C

Sex _____   Age _____

People may try a number of strategies to persuade a potential sex partner to use a condom in order to provide protection against sexually transmitted diseases (STDs). Read each of the six strategies below. Then indicate how effective you think the strategy would be and how comfortable you would feel using each strategy.

1. Promising a reward (for example, how happy you would be, or how the relationship would be improved).

1	2	3	4	5	6	7
Very ineffective						Very effective

1	2	3	4	5	6	7
Very uncomfortable						Very comfortable

2. Using emotional threats (for example, how angry and hurt you would be).

1	2	3	4	5	6	7
Very ineffective						Very effective

1	2	3	4	5	6	7
Very uncomfortable						Very comfortable

3. Providing information about the health risks of STDs.

1	2	3	4	5	6	7
Very ineffective						Very effective

1	2	3	4	5	6	7
Very uncomfortable						Very comfortable

4. Using deception or making up a different reason (like fear of pregnancy).

1	2	3	4	5	6	7
Very ineffective						Very effective

1	2	3	4	5	6	7
Very uncomfortable						Very comfortable

5. Using seduction (for example, getting your partner aroused, putting on the condom as a part of sex play).

      1   2   3   4   5   6   7
Very ineffective   Very effective

      1   2   3   4   5   6   7
Very uncomfortable   Very comfortable

6. Withholding sex (saying "no condom, no sex").

      1   2   3   4   5   6   7
Very ineffective   Very effective

      1   2   3   4   5   6   7
Very uncomfortable   Very comfortable

The last two questions concern your beliefs about heterosexual men and women's attitudes toward condoms.

7. Who do you think is more likely to encourage the use of a condom? (circle one):

     Men   Women   Both equally likely

8. Who do you think is more likely to avoid using a condom? (circle one):

     Men   Women   Both equally likely

Participant D

Sex _____   Age _____

People may try a number of strategies to persuade a potential sex partner to use a condom in order to provide protection against sexually transmitted diseases (STDs). Read each of the six strategies below. Then indicate how effective you think the strategy would be and how comfortable you would feel using each strategy.

1. Promising a reward (for example, how happy you would be, or how the relationship would be improved).

       1   2   3   4   5   6   7
Very ineffective   Very effective

       1   2   3   4   5   6   7
Very uncomfortable   Very comfortable

2. Using emotional threats (for example, how angry and hurt you would be).

       1   2   3   4   5   6   7
Very ineffective   Very effective

       1   2   3   4   5   6   7
Very uncomfortable   Very comfortable

3. Providing information about the health risks of STDs.

       1   2   3   4   5   6   7
Very ineffective   Very effective

       1   2   3   4   5   6   7
Very uncomfortable   Very comfortable

4. Using deception or making up a different reason (like fear of pregnancy).

       1   2   3   4   5   6   7
Very ineffective   Very effective

       1   2   3   4   5   6   7
Very uncomfortable   Very comfortable

5.   Using seduction (for example, getting your partner aroused, putting on the condom as a part of sex play).

1	2	3	4	5	6	7
Very ineffective						Very effective

1	2	3	4	5	6	7
Very uncomfortable						Very comfortable

6.   Withholding sex (saying "no condom, no sex").

1	2	3	4	5	6	7
Very ineffective						Very effective

1	2	3	4	5	6	7
Very uncomfortable						Very comfortable

The last two questions concern your beliefs about heterosexual men and women's attitudes toward condoms.

7.   Who do you think is more likely to encourage the use of a condom? (circle one):

Men   Women   Both equally likely

8.   Who do you think is more likely to avoid using a condom? (circle one):

Men   Women   Both equally likely

PROJECT 8.5

PUBERTY AND THE DEVELOPMENT OF SEXUALITY

Purpose: This exercise is designed to review the physiological changes associated with puberty. It also is designed to have you consider issues of adolescent and adult sexuality and personal values.

Instructions: Consider this scenario. You are the parent of two children, a 10-year-old girl and a 12-year-old boy. (Just in case you would prefer having the option of a child-free adulthood, you might want to consider these children to be your niece and nephew!) Now is the time to discuss the physiological and psychological changes associated with puberty.

1. What physical changes would you discuss with each child? How would you explain menarche? How would you explain nocturnal emissions?

2. How would you address the matter of fertility? Would you discuss different issues with each child?

3. How would you address the children's experiences of their own sexuality?

4. How would you discuss sexual orientation?

5. Would you discuss birth control and STDs? Why or why not?

6. Can you think of *one* question each child might ask that would be the most difficult to answer? What would that be?

Adapted from: Charlesworth, John R., & Slate, John R. (1986). Teaching about puberty: Learning to talk about sensitive topics. *Teaching of psychology, 13,* 215–217.

PROJECT 8.6

SEX, AGGRESSION, AND MUSIC VIDEOS: A CONTENT ANALYSIS

Purpose: This exercise is a partial replication of a study conducted by Rita Sommers-Flanagan, John Sommers-Flanagan, and Britta Davis (1993). It is designed to examine power relationships and gender roles in music videos.

Instructions: Research has begun to focus on the aggressive and sexual content in rock music videos. Whereas music videos do not contain the explicit sexuality that characterizes pornography, many of the same harmful messages are contained in this medium.

For this project you will need to watch one hour of music videos on a station such as MTV, BET, or VH-1. Using the data sheet on the following page, analyze the videos according to the coding system outlined below. Indicate the number of occurrences represented by each category. For each category, code the sex of the actor and the sex of the recipient.

Dominance: Code the power relationships. Place a check under the appropriate column for each occurrence of men and women exercising power (actors) or being subservient (recipients).

Implicit Aggression: This category includes scenes suggestive of aggression or including pain and/or threat. The use of "before and after" scenes are commonly used to imply off-camera violence. A room might be shown in disarray or a victim of aggression might be shown crying or cowering.

Explicit Aggression: In contrast to off-camera aggression this category includes filmed acts such as slapping, pushing, etc., that are intended to harm another.

Aggression with Sexuality: This category includes aggression that is sexualized. Examples might include instances where a target of aggression responds in a sexual way or is seen to enjoy aggressive sex.

Objectification: Objectification usually involves focusing on body parts (e.g., stalking legs or undulating torsos) rather than the entire person. Head shots or shots of the upper body and the face would not be included.

Implicit Sexuality: This category excludes explicit sexual activity but includes acts such as licking of lips, suggestive dancing, stroking, etc.

Explicit Sexuality: This category includes explicit sexual touch (e.g., touching breasts or genitals) or simulated sexual activity.

Music Videos Coding Sheet

Category	Male Actor	Female Actor	Male Recipient	Female Recipient
Dominance				
Implicit Aggression				
Explicit Aggression				
Aggression with Sexuality				
Objectification				
Implicit Sexuality				
Explicit Sexuality				
Totals				
Percentages				

After collecting your data, summarize your results by answering the questions on the next page.

1.   Sommers-Flanagan and her colleagues found that men were more frequently engaged in dominant and aggressive behavior than were women. Compare and contrast your results with these findings.

2.   Sommers-Flanagan and her colleagues found that women were more frequently depicted as recipients of implicit aggressive behavior, sexual behavior (both implicit and explicit), and sexually aggressive behavior. Compare and contrast your results with these findings.

3.   Consider the research in your text about the relationship between exposure to sexual and aggressive material in the media and sexual attitudes and behavior. What themes do rock videos have in common with erotica and pornography?

4.   What guidelines would you suggest for parents of adolescents who frequently watch music videos?

Reference: Sommers-Flanagan, Rita, Sommers-Flanagan, John, & Davis, Britta (1993). What's happening on music television? A gender role content analysis. *Sex Roles*, *11/12*, 745–753.

CHAPTER 9

ATTACHMENT AND INTIMACY

PROJECT 9.1

GENDER DIFFERENCES AND SIMILARITIES IN ADULT FRIENDSHIPS: CAN WOMEN AND MEN BE BEST FRIENDS?

Purpose: This exercise is designed to evaluate the nature of same-sex and cross-sex friendships in adulthood.

Instructions: Using the data sheets on the following pages, interview four adults about their friends and their understanding of friendship. Recruit two women and two men who are willing to complete a short questionnaire. Select a variety of participants for this project. Include four people who vary not only by sex but by other social categories (for example, age, race or ethnicity, sexual orientation, social class, etc.). Describe each participant by indicating her or his sex, age, and social attributes (for example, race or ethnicity, social class, etc.) at the top of each interview form.

Then, summarize your findings by answering the following questions.

1.   Compare and contrast your participants' responses to the research discussed in the text. Do your findings support the research findings? How? Are any responses inconsistent with the research? How would you explain this?

2. What do you conclude? How are men and women's cross-sex and same-sex friendships similar? How do they differ?

3. Elkins and Peterson (1993) found that a substantial proportion of college-aged women (45%) and men (47%) identified their romantic partners as their best friends. Were your results similar?

Reference: Elkins, Leigh E., & Peterson, Christopher (1993). Gender differences in best friendships. *Sex Roles, 29*, 497–508.

Participant A

Sex _____ Age _____

Characteristics/Comments_____

This survey asks you to describe two of your closest friendships. The questions will ask you about your relationship with your best female friend and your best male friend. Think for a minute about these two friends, then answer the following questions by circling the appropriate response.

1. How often do you share your personal problems and feelings with your friends?

    Female friend: 1   2   3   4   5   6   7
               Seldom   Always

    Male friend: 1   2   3   4   5   6   7
               Seldom   Always

2. How well would you say your friends know the "real you"?

    Female friend: 1   2   3   4   5   6   7
           Not very well   Extremely well

    Male friend: 1   2   3   4   5   6   7
           Not very well   Extremely well

3. How would you describe these two relationships?

    Female friend: 1   2   3   4   5   6   7
              Casual   Very intimate

    Male friend: 1   2   3   4   5   6   7
             Casual   Very intimate

4. How do you feel about these two relationships?

    Female friend: 1   2   3   4   5   6   7
          Very dissatisfied   Very satisfied

    Male friend: 1   2   3   4   5   6   7
          Very dissatisfied   Very satisfied

5. Are you romantically involved with your female friend?   Yes   No

6. Are you romantically involved with your male friend?   Yes   No

Participant B

Sex _____   Age _____

Characteristics/Comments_____

This survey asks you to describe two of your closest friendships. The questions will ask you about your relationship with your best female friend and your best male friend. Think for a minute about these two friends, then answer the following questions by circling the appropriate response.

1. How often do you share your personal problems and feelings with your friends?
    Female friend: 1   2   3   4   5   6   7
                       Seldom   Always

    Male friend: 1   2   3   4   5   6   7
                       Seldom   Always

2. How well would you say your friends know the "real you"?
    Female friend: 1   2   3   4   5   6   7
                    Not very well   Extremely well

    Male friend: 1   2   3   4   5   6   7
                    Not very well   Extremely well

3. How would you describe these two relationships?
    Female friend: 1   2   3   4   5   6   7
                       Casual   Very intimate

    Male friend: 1   2   3   4   5   6   7
                       Casual   Very intimate

4. How do you feel about these two relationships?
    Female friend: 1   2   3   4   5   6   7
                    Very dissatisfied   Very satisfied

    Male friend: 1   2   3   4   5   6   7
                    Very dissatisfied   Very satisfied

5. Are you romantically involved with your female friend?   Yes   No

6. Are you romantically involved with your male friend?   Yes   No

Participant C

Sex _____   Age _____

Characteristics/Comments_____

This survey asks you to describe two of your closest friendships. The questions will ask you about your relationship with your best female friend and your best male friend. Think for a minute about these two friends, then answer the following questions by circling the appropriate response.

1.   How often do you share your personal problems and feelings with your friends?
     Female friend: 1   2   3   4   5   6   7
                    Seldom   Always

     Male friend: 1   2   3   4   5   6   7
                    Seldom   Always

2.   How well would you say your friends know the "real you"?
     Female friend: 1   2   3   4   5   6   7
                    Not very well   Extremely well

     Male friend: 1   2   3   4   5   6   7
                    Not very well   Extremely well

3.   How would you describe these two relationships?
     Female friend: 1   2   3   4   5   6   7
                    Casual   Very intimate

     Male friend: 1   2   3   4   5   6   7
                    Casual   Very intimate

4.   How do you feel about these two relationships?
     Female friend: 1   2   3   4   5   6   7
                    Very dissatisfied   Very satisfied

     Male friend: 1   2   3   4   5   6   7
                    Very dissatisfied   Very satisfied

5.   Are you romantically involved with your female friend?   Yes   No

6.   Are you romantically involved with your male friend?   Yes   No

Participant D

Sex _____   Age _____

Characteristics/Comments_____

This survey asks you to describe two of your closest friendships. The questions will ask you about your relationship with your best female friend and your best male friend. Think for a minute about these two friends, then answer the following questions by circling the appropriate response.

1. How often do you share your personal problems and feelings with your friends?

    Female friend: 1   2   3   4   5   6   7
                    Seldom   Always

    Male friend: 1   2   3   4   5   6   7
                    Seldom   Always

2. How well would you say your friends know the "real you"?

    Female friend: 1   2   3   4   5   6   7
                    Not very well   Extremely well

    Male friend: 1   2   3   4   5   6   7
                    Not very well   Extremely well

3. How would you describe these two relationships?

    Female friend: 1   2   3   4   5   6   7
                    Casual   Very intimate

    Male friend: 1   2   3   4   5   6   7
                    Casual   Very intimate

4. How do you feel about these two relationships?

    Female friend: 1   2   3   4   5   6   7
                    Very dissatisfied   Very satisfied

    Male friend: 1   2   3   4   5   6   7
                    Very dissatisfied   Very satisfied

5. Are you romantically involved with your female friend?   Yes   No

6. Are you romantically involved with your male friend?   Yes   No

PROJECT 9.2

A CONTENT ANALYSIS OF PERSONAL ADVERTISEMENTS: THE EFFECTS OF GENDER AND SEXUAL ORIENTATION

Purpose: This exercise is a replication of a content analysis of personal ads. It is designed to compare and contrast the characteristics offered and requested by homosexual and heterosexual men and women.

Instructions: Collect one week's worth of personal ads from your local newspaper or other periodical. Make sure that ads for heterosexual and homosexual men and women are represented.

Before coding each ad, familiarize yourself with the coding categories used by Gonzales and Meyers (1993) in their original study.

Attractiveness: This category includes any mention of attributes related to physical attractiveness such as body build, beauty, eye color, slimness, etc.

Financial Security: This involves mention of financial stability and success such as professional occupation, career, home ownership, etc.

Expressiveness: This category includes traits usually associated with women and femininity in this culture, including emotional responsiveness, nurturance, caring, etc.

Instrumentality: This category includes traits usually associated with men and masculinity in this culture, including competitiveness, achievement orientation, dominance, etc.

Sincerity: Mentions of a committed, monogamous relationship are included in this category. The authors of this study also included terms such as faithful, and one-woman man.

Sexual References: This category includes references to preferences for specific sexual acts or roles, physical contact, sexual fantasies, and the like.

Sort your ads into four categories (homosexual men, heterosexual men, and homosexual women, and heterosexual women). Then, using the data sheets on the following pages code each category of ad twice. First, code the characteristics offered by the advertiser (how they describe themselves), then code the characteristics sought by the advertiser (what they're looking for) on the respective coding sheets. Make a hatch mark in the appropriate box for each mention of the characteristic in an ad. Then, summarize your findings by answering the questions at the end of the exercise.

Data Coding Sheet: Characteristics Offered

Characteristics	Homosexuals		Heterosexuals	
	Men	Women	Men	Women
Attractiveness				
Financial Security				
Expressiveness				
Instrumentality				
Sincerity				
Sexual References				

Data Coding Sheet: Characteristics Sought

Characteristics	Homosexuals		Heterosexuals	
	Men	Women	Men	Women
Attractiveness				
Financial Security				
Expressiveness				
Instrumentality				
Sincerity				
Sexual References				

1.   Summarize your data. What patterns did you find?

2.   Compare your results to the research in your text.

      What attributes do men (regardless of sexual orientation) offer/seek?

      What attributes do women (regardless of sexual orientation) offer/seek?

3. A consistent finding in the literature is that physical attractiveness is an important factor in interpersonal attraction and mate selection. Did you find physical attractiveness was equally important for all groups? Were there differences as a function of gender and/or sexual orientation?

4. Simon Davis (1990) found that traditional gender-role stereotypes were reflected in personal ads. He found that men were described as "success objects" and women as "sex objects." What were your findings?

5. Compare and contrast your findings to the research in your text on gender and sexual orientation, interpersonal attraction, sexual behavior, and sexual attitudes.

References: Davis, Simon. (1990). Men as success objects and women as sex objects: A study of personal advertisements. *Sex Roles, 23*, 43–50.

Gonzales, Marti H., & Meyers, Sarah A. (1993). "Your mother would like me": Self-presentation in the personals ads of heterosexual and homosexual men and women. *Personality and Social Psychology Bulletin, 19*, 131–142.

PROJECT 9.3

SINGLEHOOD: BY CIRCUMSTANCE OR BY CHOICE?

Purpose: The purpose of this exercise is to consider the experiences of women and men who are not married or cohabiting with a partner.

Instructions: Review the research in your text in the areas of interpersonal relationships, marriage, and commitment. You are likely to find that single adults are rarely mentioned. The establishment and maintenance of a primary relationship in adulthood is a common expectation in this culture, and most people spend much of their adult lives in a committed relationship with a partner. On the other hand, many men and women spend their adult years as single adults. This diverse category includes people in a number of circumstances.

Using the interview schedule that follows, interview a friend, family member, or acquaintance who has been single most of his or her adult life. Briefly describe your respondent (e.g., race or ethnicity, number and ages of any children, sexual orientation, etc.) at the heading of the schedule, and ask her or him to respond to each of the interview questions. Then, compare your findings to the material in the text on interpersonal relationships, intimacy, and attachment in adulthood.

Summarize your findings by responding to the questions below.

1. Some demographic factors are predictive of single status. For example, heterosexual African American women are more likely to remain single due to the fact they outnumber African American men in adulthood. Also, better-educated women with prestigious or well-paying jobs are more likely to remain single. Were any of these factors cited by your respondent? If so, what were they?

2. Single women may be stereotyped as spinsters or old maids. Single men may be stereotyped as swinging playboys or fussy, perhaps, gay men. Did your respondent discuss being stigmatized by such stereotypes?

3. How important is work to your respondent? What role does work play in his or her life?

4. Comment on your respondent's social network and relationships with others. Compare and contrast this information with the text's discussion of married or cohabiting couples.

Interview Schedule

Sex_____   Age_____

Comments/Characteristics_____

_____

1. Who do you consider to be "family"? With whom do you spend holidays, birthdays, and other special events?

2. What do you do for a living? Do you enjoy your work? Would you consider yourself to have a job or a career?

3. Do people ever ask you why you never married? If they do, what do you say?

4.   What are the *best* things about being single?

5.   What are the *worst* things about being single?

6.   Very little social science research has been conducted on single adults. If you had your say, what aspect of being single should social scientists study? Why?

PROJECT 9.4

WORK FOR PAY AND WORK IN THE HOME: WHO DOES THE HOUSEWORK?

Purpose: This exercise is an assessment of the division of household labor between a married or cohabiting couple.

Instructions: Using the data sheets at the end of this exercise, interview two people who live together in a domestic partnership. Both should be employed at least part-time. First, have each of your respondents describe themselves and their employment situations by answering the questions on the Couple Description Form. Then interview each of them individually about how they share household chores and child care using the Household Responsibilities Survey.

Summarize your interview by reviewing the text's material on the division of labor, family responsibilities, and paid employment, and then answer the questions below.

1. Arlie Hochschild (1989) coined the term "the second shift" to characterize the fact that women put in almost another 40 hours per week on housework after working on the job. Compare and contrast your findings. How equitable is the division of labor in this instance?

2. If the couple has children, how did their presence affect the division of labor?

3. How did your respondents divide up chores? For example, was it along the lines of perceived competence? Traditional gender lines?

4. Did the type of job (that is, paid employment) held by each partner affect the division of labor? If so, how?

5. Can you comment on any factors that seemed to lead to problems in the division of labor? At the same time, were there any factors that seemed to contribute to satisfaction with the division of labor?

Reference: Hochschild, Arlie (1989). *The second shift*. New York: Avon.

Couple Description Form

Partner A

Age _____   Sex _____

Occupation_____

On the average, how many hours per week do you work?   _____

On the average, how many hours per week do you commute?_____

Other comments_____

_____

_____

Partner B

Age _____   Sex _____

Occupation_____

On the average, how many hours per week do you work?   _____

On the average, how many hours per week do you commute?_____

Other comments_____

_____

_____

Household Responsibilities Survey

1. How have you and your partner divided up the housework (e.g., making beds, cleaning, dusting, etc.)?

    Partner A:

    Partner B:

2. How have you and your partner divided up the yard work (e.g., mowing the lawn, weeding, etc.)?

    Partner A:

    Partner B:

3.   What arrangements have you and your partner made for household repairs (e.g., fixing plumbing, painting, etc.)?

Partner A:

Partner B:

4.   (Ask only if the couple has children.) What arrangements have you and your partner made for child care (e.g., feeding, basic care, supervision, transportation, etc.)?

Partner A:

Partner B:

5. Who is responsible for keeping track of social responsibilities (e.g., remembering to buy and send birthday cards and gifts, planning anniversary parties, etc.)?

   Partner A:

   Partner B:

6. Do you rely upon hired help (e.g., housekeepers, gardeners, etc.)? For which chores or tasks?

   Partner A:

   Partner B:

7.   How did the two of you work out your arrangement? How did you divide up the work that needed to be done?

Partner A:

Partner B:

8.   (Ask only if the couple has children.) What adjustments, if any, did becoming parents require you to make?

Partner A:

Partner B:

9.   What seems to work best about your arrangement? What doesn't seem to work?

Partner A:

Partner B:

PROJECT 9.5

SOCIAL SUPPORT AND INTERPERSONAL RELATIONSHIPS: A VISIT TO A SELF-HELP GROUP

Purpose: This exercise requires that you visit and evaluate a self-help group.

Instructions: The self-help movement has experienced huge growth during the last decade. Self-help groups have proliferated among those who feel traditional psychotherapy might not meet their needs in coping with interpersonal problems. These groups provide social support, an important factor in physical and mental health.

Identify a self-help group that targets an area in which you are interested. This could include groups that are organized around helping people cope with family members' problems (e.g., Ala-Non), or life transitions (e.g., Parents Without Partners), or general social support groups (e.g., Parents and Friends of Lesbians and Gays). Consult your campus and community mental health center, telephone directory, and library to find a location and meeting time for the organization. Attend one meeting and evaluate the organization.

Remember—it is important to respect and protect the anonymity of any participants in your report.

1. Which group did you visit? What is the group's focus?

2. Self-help groups can provide two important facets of social support. These include information that is helpful in coping (e.g., tips for avoiding alcohol cravings) and emotional support (e.g., a confidant with a similar problem). How would you judge the group's ability to provide both types of support?

3. The self-help movement has been criticized for overuse of the concept of codependency. This involves a pattern of dysfunctional relationships within the family that "enables" the family member continue her or his problem behavior. Although there is little evidence for this concept (and some argue that it pathologizes women's role within their families), many groups focus on codependency and enablers within the family. Describe any discussion of dysfunctional relationships that you observed.

4. Overall, how would you evaluate the usefulness of this group? Relate your findings to the text and course material.

CHAPTER 10

PARENTING AND OTHER FAMILY TIES

PROJECT 10.1

INTERGENERATIONAL RELATIONSHIPS

Purpose: This exercise requires you to interview with a couple about their relationships with older and younger family members. It is designed to assess the ways in which family relationships may change with age.

Instructions: Recruit a couple who have had at least one adult child. You may conduct joint or individual interviews; separate worksheets are provided for each participant. Complete the descriptive information at the top of each worksheet, including a summary of demographic characteristics such as race/ethnicity, social class, or sexual orientation.

After you have completed the worksheets, summarize your results by answering the questions below.

1. Compare and contrast your participants' remarks to the research in your text on parenting, launching of children in adulthood, and grandparenting.

2. Did you find any evidence of "empty nest syndrome"? How did they deal with their changing roles as parents?

3. Middle-aged adults have been referred to as the "sandwich generation." People in this age group (especially women) often experience pressure to support adult children and aging parents. Comment on your participants' relationships with both generations.

4. If you interviewed a heterosexual couple, were the issues raised in the previous questions perceived differently by your male and female respondents? Or did you observe more similarities than differences?

Participant A

Sex _____ Age_____

Comments/Characteristics_____

1. How many children do you have (including stepchildren)? How many sons? Daughters? How old are they?

2. Do any of your children still live with you? Where do the rest of your children live?

3. How often do you see your children?

4. Now that your children are grown, have any of your relationships changed? Do you spend more time with your partner or friends, for example? Do you do different things?

5. Do you have any grandchildren? If so, how does it feel to be a grandparent?

6. Are your parents still living? If so, how old are they? Where do they live?

7. How often do you see your parents? Do they rely upon you for financial or social support? If so, describe.

8. In what ways has your relationship with your parents changed? How has it remained the same?

Participant B

Sex _____   Age_____

Comments/Characteristics_____

1. How many children do you have (including stepchildren)? How many sons? Daughters? How old are they?

2. Do any of your children still live with you? Where do the rest of your children live?

3. How often do you see your children?

4. Now that your children are grown, have any of your relationships changed? Do you spend more time with your partner or friends, for example? Do you do different things?

5.   Do you have any grandchildren? If so, how does it feel to be a grandparent?

6.   Are your parents still living? If so, how old are they? Where do they live?

7.   How often do you see your parents? Do they rely upon you for financial or social support? If so, describe.

8.   In what ways has your relationship with your parents changed? How has it remained the same?

PROJECT 10.2

BALANCING MULTIPLE ROLES

Purpose: This exercise is designed to have you consider changing trends in the configuration of family and gender roles.

Instructions: Interview two couples who are willing to describe how they have balanced their work and family lives. One couple should be young adults, the other should be middle-aged or older adults. Both should have children. Two different generations from the same family would be ideal candidates for this project. You may conduct joint or individual interviews; separate worksheets are provided for each participant. Describe each participant at the top of each worksheet. Also include any other relevant factors such as race or ethnicity and social class.

Compare their experiences with reference to the text by responding to the following questions.

1. Compare and contrast the couples' responses. What similarities did you observe between genders or couples? What differences did you observe?

2. How did your participants juggle work and family? Did having children affect women and men similarly? What gender differences, if any, did you find?

3.   Did you find evidence of a "mommy track" in employment? Did men work longer hours to meet increased financial obligations?

4.   Compare and contrast your participants' descriptions of their experience in juggling work and parenting. Describe any age or gender differences you observed in parenting ideology.

Work and Family Survey

Participant A

Sex _____   Age _____

Number and Ages of Children_____

Comments/Characteristics_____

1. Did becoming parents change the way you related to each other? If so, how did your relationship change?

2. How did becoming pregnant and then raising your children affect the family's finances?

3. Were you employed at the time your first child was born? How did becoming a parent change things? For example, did you work longer hours? Or did you switch to a part-time job after staying home with your children?

4. Did having children affect your education in any way? For example, did you decide to take classes when your children were old enough to enter school? Or, did you have to postpone or interrupt your education?

5. Think for a minute about your experience raising your children.

    When was it most satisfying being a parent? How old were your children at the time?

    When was it most stressful being a parent? How old were your children at the time?

Work and Family Survey

Participant B

Sex _____   Age _____

Number and Ages of Children_____

Comments/Characteristics_____

1. Did becoming parents change the way you related to each other? If so, how did your relationship change?

2. How did becoming pregnant and then raising your children affect the family's finances?

3. Were you employed at the time your first child was born? How did becoming a parent change things? For example, did you work longer hours? Or did you switch to a part-time job after staying home with your children?

4.   Did having children affect your education in any way? For example, did you decide to take classes when your children were old enough to enter school? Or, did you have to postpone or interrupt your education?

5.   Think for a minute about your experience raising your children.

     When was it most satisfying being a parent? How old were your children at the time?

     When was it most stressful being a parent? How old were your children at the time?

Work and Family Survey

Participant C

Sex _____   Age _____

Number and Ages of Children_____

Comments/Characteristics_____

1.   Did becoming parents change the way you related to each other? If so,
      how did your relationship change?

2.   How did becoming pregnant and then raising your children affect the
      family's finances?

3.   Were you employed at the time your first child was born? How did
      becoming a parent change things? For example, did you work longer
      hours? Or did you switch to a part-time job after staying home with your
      children?

4. Did having children affect your education in any way? For example, did you decide to take classes when your children were old enough to enter school? Or, did you have to postpone or interrupt your education?

5. Think for a minute about your experience raising your children.

When was it most satisfying being a parent? How old were your children at the time?

When was it most stressful being a parent? How old were your children at the time?

Work and Family Survey

Participant D

Sex _____   Age _____

Number and Ages of Children_____

Comments/Characteristics_____

1. Did becoming parents change the way you related to each other? If so, how did your relationship change?

2. How did becoming pregnant and then raising your children affect the family's finances?

3. Were you employed at the time your first child was born? How did becoming a parent change things? For example, did you work longer hours? Or did you switch to a part-time job after staying home with your children?

4. Did having children affect your education in any way? For example, did you decide to take classes when your children were old enough to enter school? Or, did you have to postpone or interrupt your education?

5. Think for a minute about your experience raising your children.

When was it most satisfying being a parent? How old were your children at the time?

When was it most stressful being a parent? How old were your children at the time?

PROJECT 10.3

CHILD CARE IN YOUR COMMUNITY

Purpose: This exercise is designed to increase your awareness of the cost, quality, and availability of child care in your community. It also is designed to have you consider the factors parents face in juggling their work responsibilities and the requirements of their child care providers.

Instructions: Find two child care facilities listed in the phone book. Call each and obtain the information on the evaluation worksheets that follow. Explain to the people you contact that you are a college student whose instructor has asked you to do a brief survey of the cost and availability of child care. Tell them that their facility will not be identified (unless they say it's OK).

Summarize your findings by answering the following questions:

1. If you were employed full time (that is, working a typical 40-hour week), would these facilities be able to provide care for the time you were at work? Could accommodations be made in the case of overtime?

2. Suppose you were employed in an entry-level position making $20,000 per year. Your take-home pay is approximately $1,250 per month. How much of a bite would child care take out of your salary? For one child? For two children?

3. Consider the cost of child care, the rewards of work, and the effect quality of child care has on children. What sort of factors would you consider in deciding whether to place your children in these facilities?

Child Care Facility Evaluation Sheet

Facility A

1. What ages of children do you accept for child care? Do you accept newborns?

2. Do you accept children who are not potty-trained?

3. What are your fees?

4. If you have a sliding scale, how are fees established by income?

5. What is the child-caretaker ratio?

6. Are staff members certified? What training do they receive?

7.   What services and supervision do you provide (for example, number of snacks or meals, play time, etc.)?

8.   During what hours may a child be left for care?

9.   If a parent might be late due to a work emergency, do you have overtime rates? How much notice is required?

10. Do you accept a child who has the sniffles or who might be coming down with a cold?

Child Care Facility Evaluation Sheet

Facility B

1. What ages of children do you accept for child care? Do you accept newborns?

2. Do you accept children who are not potty-trained?

3. What are your fees?

4. If you have a sliding scale, how are fees established by income?

5. What is the child-caretaker ratio?

6. Are staff members certified? What training do they receive?

7. What services and supervision do you provide (for example, number of snacks or meals, play time, etc.)?

8. During what hours may a child be left for care?

9. If a parent might be late due to a work emergency, do you have overtime rates? How much notice is required?

10. Do you accept a child who has the sniffles or who might be coming down with a cold?

PROJECT 10.4

A CHILLY CLIMATE FOR FATHERS?

Purpose: This exercise is designed to have you investigate attitudes toward mothers and fathers taking parental leave when a child is born.

Instructions: American fathers have not taken advantage of parental leave. For example, recent studies indicate that approximately 1% of all eligible male workers use the leave to which they are entitled. Louise Silverstein (1996) argues that negative attitudes in the workplace may discourage fathers from taking parental leave.

Using the interview formats on the following pages, interview two men and two women. Notice that two versions of the interview format have been prepared. Ask one of your male participants to evaluate "Steve" and the other to evaluate "Susan." Similarly, one female participant should evaluate "Steve" and the other "Susan."

Select a variety of participants for this project. Include four people who vary not only by sex but by other social categories (for example, age, race or ethnicity, sexual orientation, social class, etc.). Be sure to describe each participant by indicating her or his sex, age, and social attributes (for example, race or ethnicity, social class, etc.) at the top of each interview form.

Summarize your findings by answering the following questions.

1. Compare and contrast your findings. Overall, were attitudes more positive toward Steve or Susan? Or were attitudes similar toward both?

2.   Silverstein hypothesizes that coworkers and supervisors may perceive men who take parental leave as being uncommitted to their jobs and unmasculine. What were your findings?

3.   Many fathers take paid sick leave or vacation time when their children are born. The majority of the respondents in the 1993 Wisconsin Maternity Leave and Health Project Study took five days or less (Hyde, Essex, & Horton, 1993). On average, how much time did your participants report was appropriate? Were there gender differences or similarities?

References: Hyde, Janet S., Essex, M. J., & Horton, F. (1993). Fathers and parental leave. *Journal of Family Issues, 15*, 616–641.

Silverstein, Louise B. (1996). Fathering is a feminist issue. *Psychology of Women Quarterly, 20*, 3–37.

Participant A

Sex _____   Age _____

Comments/Characteristics_____

Steve Lee has been employed as a software developer for five years. He is a member of a development team that has been working closely together on a new product that will ship in six months. The team is under a great deal of pressure from management to meet a number of deadlines. Steve's wife has just given birth to their first child. Her pregnancy and childbirth were free of medical complications. Steve has requested that his supervisor grant him parental leave. He has accumulated vacation and sick pay.

1. How would you evaluate Steve as a father?

       1   2   3   4   5   6   7

  Very negative   Very positive

2. How would you evaluate Steve as a coworker?

       1   2   3   4   5   6   7

  Very negative   Very positive

3. How would you evaluate Steve as a man?

       1   2   3   4   5   6   7

  Not at all masculine   Very masculine

4. Rate the level of commitment you feel that Steve has for his job.

       1   2   3   4   5   6   7

  Very low   Very high

5. I feel that Steve should use sick pay or vacation time for his leave.

       1   2   3   4   5   6   7

  Strongly disagree   Strongly agree

6. I feel that Steve should receive unpaid parental leave.

       1   2   3   4   5   6   7

  Strongly disagree   Strongly agree

7. In your opinion, how many days off should Steve receive? _____

Participant B

Sex _____   Age _____

Comments/Characteristics_____

Steve Lee has been employed as a software developer for five years. He is a member of a development team that has been working closely together on a new product that will ship in six months. The team is under a great deal of pressure from management to meet a number of deadlines. Steve's wife has just given birth to their first child. Her pregnancy and childbirth were free of medical complications. Steve has requested that his supervisor grant him parental leave. He has accumulated vacation and sick pay.

1.   How would you evaluate Steve as a father?
         1   2   3   4   5   6   7
   Very negative   Very positive

2.   How would you evaluate Steve as a coworker?
         1   2   3   4   5   6   7
   Very negative   Very positive

3.   How would you evaluate Steve as a man?
         1   2   3   4   5   6   7
 Not at all masculine   Very masculine

4.   Rate the level of commitment you feel that Steve has for his job.
         1   2   3   4   5   6   7
   Very low   Very high

5.   I feel that Steve should use sick pay or vacation time for his leave.
         1   2   3   4   5   6   7
 Strongly disagree   Strongly agree

6.   I feel that Steve should receive unpaid parental leave.
         1   2   3   4   5   6   7
 Strongly disagree   Strongly agree

7.   In your opinion, how many days off should Steve receive?   _____

Participant C

Sex _____   Age _____

Comments/Characteristics_____

Susan Lee has been employed as a software developer for five years. She is a member of a development team that has been working closely together on a new product that will ship in six months. The team is under a great deal of pressure from management to meet a number of deadlines. Susan has just given birth to her first child. Her pregnancy and childbirth were free of medical complications. Susan has requested that her supervisor grant her parental leave. She has accumulated vacation and sick pay.

1. How would you evaluate Susan as a mother?
       1   2   3   4   5   6   7
    Very negative   Very positive

2. How would you evaluate Susan as a coworker?
       1   2   3   4   5   6   7
    Very negative   Very positive

3. How would you evaluate Susan as a woman?
       1   2   3   4   5   6   7
    Not at all feminine   Very feminine

4. Rate the level of commitment you feel that Susan has for her job.
       1   2   3   4   5   6   7
    Very low   Very high

5. I feel that Susan should use sick pay or vacation time for her leave.
       1   2   3   4   5   6   7
    Strongly disagree   Strongly agree

6. I feel that Susan should receive unpaid parental leave.
       1   2   3   4   5   6   7
    Strongly disagree   Strongly agree

7. In your opinion, how many days off should Susan receive? _____

Participant D

Sex _____   Age _____

Comments/Characteristics _____

Susan Lee has been employed as a software developer for five years. She is a member of a development team that has been working closely together on a new product that will ship in six months. The team is under a great deal of pressure from management to meet a number of deadlines. Susan has just given birth to her first child. Her pregnancy and childbirth were free of medical complications. Susan has requested that her supervisor grant her parental leave. She has accumulated vacation and sick pay.

1.   How would you evaluate Susan as a mother?
        1   2   3   4   5   6   7
     Very negative   Very positive

2.   How would you evaluate Susan as a coworker?
        1   2   3   4   5   6   7
     Very negative   Very positive

3.   How would you evaluate Susan as a woman?
        1   2   3   4   5   6   7
     Not at all feminine   Very feminine

4.   Rate the level of commitment you feel that Susan has for her job.
        1   2   3   4   5   6   7
     Very low   Very high

5.   I feel that Susan should use sick pay or vacation time for her leave.
        1   2   3   4   5   6   7
     Strongly disagree   Strongly agree

6.   I feel that Susan should receive unpaid parental leave.
        1   2   3   4   5   6   7
     Strongly disagree   Strongly agree

7.   In your opinion, how many days off should Susan receive?   _____

CHAPTER 11

PHYSICAL AND MENTAL HEALTH

PROJECT 11.1

GENDER AND HEALTH-RELATED BEHAVIORS

Purpose: This exercise is designed to have you investigate gender differences in health-enhancing (e.g., engaging in preventive medical care, maintaining a healthful diet and exercise regimen, taking steps to avoid accidents and serious injury, etc.) and health-compromising (e.g., excessive alcohol consumption, cigarette smoking, driving recklessly or without a seatbelt, etc.) behaviors.

Instructions: Using the questionnaires on the following pages, recruit two men and two women who are willing to discuss their health-related behaviors. Select a variety of participants for this project. Be sure to describe each participant by indicating her or his sex, age, and social attributes (for example, race or ethnicity, social class, etc.) at the top of each interview form.

Summarize your results by answering the following questions.

1. In general, women have been found to engage in more health-enhancing behaviors than men. Compare and contrast your findings.

2. Men and women also differ in the extent to which they engage in behavior that is risky to their health. In fact, Harrison, Chin, and Ficarrotto (1995) assert that "masculinity may be dangerous to your health." Compare and contrast your findings.

3.   Consider the gender differences in mortality (death) and morbidity (illness) rates reported in your text. How might gender differences in health-related behaviors contribute to these differences?

4.   Based upon your findings, how would you say gender influences lifestyle factors that are related to health and illness?

Refrence: Harrison, James, Chin, James, & Ficarrotto, Thomas. (1995). Warning: Masculinity can be dangerous to your health. In M. Kimmel & M. Messner (Eds.), *Men's lives* (3rd ed.) (pp. 237–249). Needham Heights, MA: Allyn & Bacon.

Physical Health Questionnaire

Sex _____   Age_____

Comments/Characteristics_____

1. How often do you engage in the following behaviors? (circle one)

   Wear sunscreen
   | 1 | 2 | 3 | 4 | 5 | 6 | 7 |
   Never   Always

   Wear seatbelts
   | 1 | 2 | 3 | 4 | 5 | 6 | 7 |
   Never   Always

   Perform a monthly breast self-exam (if female) or testicular self-exam
   (if male)
   | 1 | 2 | 3 | 4 | 5 | 6 | 7 |
   Never   Always

   Eat foods that are high in fat and calories
   | 1 | 2 | 3 | 4 | 5 | 6 | 7 |
   Never   Always

   Smoke cigarettes
   | 1 | 2 | 3 | 4 | 5 | 6 | 7 |
   Never   Always

   Drink alcoholic beverages
   | 1 | 2 | 3 | 4 | 5 | 6 | 7 |
   Never   Always

   Engage in physical exercise
   | 1 | 2 | 3 | 4 | 5 | 6 | 7 |
   Never   Always

2. Do you have a primary physician who you see on a regular basis? _____

3. How long has it been since your last medical checkup? _____

4. Would you say that you know at least one person who you can talk with about things that are important to you? _____

Physical Health Questionnaire

Sex   _____   Age_____

Comments/Characteristics_____

1. How often do you engage in the following behaviors? (circle one)

    Wear sunscreen
    | 1 | 2 | 3 | 4 | 5 | 6 | 7 |
    | Never | | | | | | Always |

    Wear seatbelts
    | 1 | 2 | 3 | 4 | 5 | 6 | 7 |
    | Never | | | | | | Always |

    Perform a monthly breast self-exam (if female) or testicular self-exam (if male)
    | 1 | 2 | 3 | 4 | 5 | 6 | 7 |
    | Never | | | | | | Always |

    Eat foods that are high in fat and calories
    | 1 | 2 | 3 | 4 | 5 | 6 | 7 |
    | Never | | | | | | Always |

    Smoke cigarettes
    | 1 | 2 | 3 | 4 | 5 | 6 | 7 |
    | Never | | | | | | Always |

    Drink alcoholic beverages
    | 1 | 2 | 3 | 4 | 5 | 6 | 7 |
    | Never | | | | | | Always |

    Engage in physical exercise
    | 1 | 2 | 3 | 4 | 5 | 6 | 7 |
    | Never | | | | | | Always |

2. Do you have a primary physician who you see on a regular basis?   _____

3. How long has it been since your last medical checkup?   _____

4. Would you say that you know at least one person who you can talk with about things that are important to you?   _____

Physical Health Questionnaire

Sex _____   Age_____

Comments/Characteristics_____

1. How often do you engage in the following behaviors? (circle one)

    Wear sunscreen
    1   2   3   4   5   6   7
    Never   Always

    Wear seatbelts
    1   2   3   4   5   6   7
    Never   Always

    Perform a monthly breast self-exam (if female) or testicular self-exam
    (if male)
    1   2   3   4   5   6   7
    Never   Always

    Eat foods that are high in fat and calories
    1   2   3   4   5   6   7
    Never   Always

    Smoke cigarettes
    1   2   3   4   5   6   7
    Never   Always

    Drink alcoholic beverages
    1   2   3   4   5   6   7
    Never   Always

    Engage in physical exercise
    1   2   3   4   5   6   7
    Never   Always

2. Do you have a primary physician who you see on a regular basis?   _____

3. How long has it been since your last medical checkup?   _____

4. Would you say that you know at least one person who you can talk with
    about things that are important to you?   _____

Physical Health Questionnaire

Sex _____   Age_____

Comments/Characteristics_____

1. How often do you engage in the following behaviors? (circle one)

Wear sunscreen
    1   2   3   4   5   6   7
Never   Always

Wear seatbelts
    1   2   3   4   5   6   7
Never   Always

Perform a monthly breast self-exam (if female) or testicular self-exam
(if male)
    1   2   3   4   5   6   7
Never   Always

Eat foods that are high in fat and calories
    1   2   3   4   5   6   7
Never   Always

Smoke cigarettes
    1   2   3   4   5   6   7
Never   Always

Drink alcoholic beverages
    1   2   3   4   5   6   7
Never   Always

Engage in physical exercise
    1   2   3   4   5   6   7
Never   Always

2. Do you have a primary physician who you see on a regular basis? _____

3. How long has it been since your last medical checkup? _____

4. Would you say that you know at least one person who you can talk with
    about things that are important to you?   _____

PROJECT 11.2

THE POLITICS OF HEALTH RESEARCH

Purpose: This exercise involves research into the current status of the Women's Health Initiative.

Instructions: Medical researchers have been criticized for systematically excluding women from medical and pharmacological research. In fact, females (humans and other species) were excluded from federally-funded studies until the mid-1980s. In response, the Office of Research on Women's Health was established as a part of the National Institutes of Health in 1991. One of its first actions was to eliminate the exclusion of women from federally-funded studies.

The NIH launched the Women's Health Initiative, a long-term study of women's health issues. Using the resources at the campus library, report on the current status of this study. Information may be found in major newspapers (e.g., *Los Angeles Times, New York Times*) and news magazines and periodicals (e.g., *Newsweek, US News and World Report*). Information also may be obtained on-line via the World Wide Web and Medline.

1. What health-related behaviors and illnesses are being studied?

2. Who are the research participants? How are they being recruited? What are the demographic characteristics of the sample?

3. What results have been reported by the news media?

4. Review your text's discussion of gender differences in mortality and morbidity rates. What questions will this study address? What questions will remain to be answered?

PROJECT 11.3

BODY IMAGE: HOW SATISFIED ARE MEN AND WOMEN WITH THEIR BODIES?

Purpose: This exercise is designed to compare men's and women's body image. It is a partial replication of research conducted by Drewnowski and Yee (1987).

Instructions: Using the data sheets on the following pages, interview two women and two men. Describe each participant by indicating his or her sex, age, and social attributes (for example, race or ethnicity, sexual orientation, or social class) at the top of the interview forms. Also indicate other relevant factors. This might include whether your respondent is pregnant, a collegiate athlete, etc.

1. Compute each respondent's Body Mass Index (BMI), which is a standard measure of a healthy weight. This involves the following steps:

    a. Compute weight in kilograms (1 kilogram = 2.2 pounds)

    b. Compute height in meters (1 meter = 39.4 inches), then square that figure

    c. Compute BMI:

    $$\frac{\text{Weight (kg)}}{\text{Height (m)}^2}$$

    d. Write this figure at the bottom of each participant's data sheet.

2. Compare each respondent's BMI to the following ranges:

	Women	Men
Aged 34 or younger	19–24	20–25
Aged 35 or older	21–26	22–27

3. Indicate next to each BMI whether the respondent is underweight, at a healthy weight, or overweight.

4.   Compare men's and women's responses to interview questions 4 and 5. Drewnowski and Yee found that women were more likely to describe themselves as overweight and to be dissatisfied with their bodies than were men. What were your findings?

5.   Compare men's and women's current and ideal body weights with the BMI ratings you computed. How accurate are their perceptions?

6.   Inspect the dieting and exercise habits of those who wish to lose weight. Men are more likely to exercise to lose weight while women are more likely to diet. What were your findings?

7. Relate your findings to the course material. How is body image related to eating disorders and compulsive exercising in men and women?

Reference: Drewnowski, Adam, & Yee, Doris K. (1987). Men and body image: Are males satisfied with their body weight? *Psychosomatic Medicine*, *49*, 626–634.

Participant A

Sex _____   Age _____

Characteristics/Comments_____

1. What is your height?   _____

2. What is your *current* weight?   _____

3. What is your *ideal* weight?   _____

4. How would you describe yourself?
        1   2   3   4   5
      Very   Underweight Average   Overweight   Very
    underweight   overweight

5. How satisfied are you with the shape of your body?
        1   2   3   4   5
      Never   Rarely   Sometimes   Often   Always

6. During the past month, how many days have you followed a reduced-
    calorie diet?
        1   2   3   4   5
      Never   1-3 days   4-7 days   1-2 weeks Over 2 weeks

7. During the past month, how many days have you followed an exercise
    program?
        1   2   3   4   5
      Never   1-3 days   4-7 days   1-2 weeks Over 2 weeks

8. During the past month, how long do you typically exercise?
        1   2   3
    Less than   30-60   More than
   30 min./session   min./session   60 min./session

Participant B

Sex _____   Age _____

Characteristics/Comments_____

1. What is your height?   _____

2. What is your *current* weight?   _____

3. What is your *ideal* weight?   _____

4. How would you describe yourself?
1	2	3	4	5
Very underweight	Underweight	Average	Overweight	Very overweight

5. How satisfied are you with the shape of your body?
1	2	3	4	5
Never	Rarely	Sometimes	Often	Always

6. During the past month, how many days have you followed a reduced-calorie diet?
1	2	3	4	5
Never	1-3 days	4-7 days	1-2 weeks	Over 2 weeks

7. During the past month, how many days have you followed an exercise program?
1	2	3	4	5
Never	1-3 days	4-7 days	1-2 weeks	Over 2 weeks

8. During the past month, how long do you typically exercise?
1	2	3
Less than 30 min./session	30-60 min./session	More than 60 min./session

Participant C

Sex _____   Age   _____

Characteristics/Comments_____

1. What is your height?   _____

2. What is your *current* weight?   _____

3. What is your *ideal* weight?   _____

4. How would you describe yourself?
    1   2   3   4   5
    Very   Underweight   Average   Overweight   Very
    underweight   overweight

5. How satisfied are you with the shape of your body?
    1   2   3   4   5
    Never   Rarely   Sometimes   Often   Always

6. During the past month, how many days have you followed a reduced-
    calorie diet?
    1   2   3   4   5
    Never   1-3 days   4-7 days   1-2 weeks   Over 2 weeks

7. During the past month, how many days have you followed an exercise
    program?
    1   2   3   4   5
    Never   1-3 days   4-7 days   1-2 weeks   Over 2 weeks

8. During the past month, how long do you typically exercise?
    1   2   3
    Less than   30-60   More than
    30 min./session   min./session   60 min./session

Participant D

Sex _____   Age _____

Characteristics/Comments_____

1. What is your height?   _____

2. What is your *current* weight?   _____

3. What is your *ideal* weight?   _____

4. How would you describe yourself?
        1   2   3   4   5
      Very   Underweight   Average   Overweight   Very
    underweight   overweight

5. How satisfied are you with the shape of your body?
        1   2   3   4   5
      Never   Rarely   Sometimes   Often   Always

6. During the past month, how many days have you followed a reduced-calorie diet?
        1   2   3   4   5
      Never   1-3 days   4-7 days   1-2 weeks Over 2 weeks

7. During the past month, how many days have you followed an exercise program?
        1   2   3   4   5
      Never   1-3 days   4-7 days   1-2 weeks Over 2 weeks

8. During the past month, how long do you typically exercise?
        1   2   3
    Less than   30-60   More than
  30 min./session   min./session   60 min./session

PROJECT 11.4

GENDER, RUMINATION, AND DEPRESSION

Purpose: This exercise is designed to explore gender differences in cognitive response styles that may be related to depression.

Instructions: Susan Nolen-Hoeksema (1990) argues that one of the factors related to the greater incidence in depression among women is differences in cognitive response styles. Men are more likely to respond to depression by engaging in activities that "get their minds off of things." She labels this a *distracting* style. In contrast, women are more likely to exhibit a *ruminative* style whereby they "mull over" their feelings and focus inward on themselves and their unhappiness.

Using the data sheets on the following pages, ask two women and two men to complete a short questionnaire on their response to depression. Describe each participant by indicating his or her sex, age, and social attributes (for example, race or ethnicity, sexual orientation, or social class) at the top of the interview forms.

1. Items 1, 4, 5, 7, 8, 10 correspond to the distracting style. Count each participant's responses to this group and write this number at the bottom of each questionnaire, labeling it *distracting*.

2. Items 2, 3, 6. 9, 11, 12 correspond to the ruminative style. Count up the number of responses that fall into this group and write this number at the bottom of each questionnaire, labeling it *ruminative*.

3. Compare the two scores. Did you find gender differences or similarities?

4. What aspects of the distracting style might be adaptive in responding to depression? What aspects might be maladaptive?

5. What aspects of the ruminative style encourage depression to linger? What aspects might be effective in reducing negative mood?

6. What is it about gender-role socialization that might contribute to gender differences in rumination and depression?

Reference: Nolen-Hoeksema, Susan (1990). *Sex differences in depression*. Stanford, CA: Stanford University Press.

Participant A

Sex _____   Age _____

Characteristics/Comments_____

Suppose that a recent personal event has put you in a depressed mood (e.g., an unexpectedly low grade on an exam, the breakup of a love relationship, or a quarrel with a close friend or relative). Check which of the following activities you are likely to engage in when you are depressed. You may check as many that apply.

_____ 1.   Working on a hobby that takes concentration.

_____ 2.   Writing in a diary about how you are feeling.

_____ 3.   Getting away from everyone else to try to sort out your emotions.

_____ 4.   Doing something with your friends.

_____ 5.   Getting drunk.

_____ 6.   Telling friends about how depressed you are.

_____ 7.   Punching something.

_____ 8.   Engaging in sports.

_____ 9.   Writing a letter to someone describing your emotions.

_____ 10. Engaging in reckless behavior (e.g., driving 10 miles over the speed limit).

_____ 11. Listening to music.

_____ 12. Making a list of the reasons you are sad or depressed.

Figure from *Psychology of Women*, (3rd. ed.), by Margaret W. Matlin, copyright © 1996 by Holt, Rinehart and Winston, Inc., adapted by permission of the publisher. Based on Nolen-Hoeksema, Susan (1990). *Sex differences in depression*. Stanford, CA: Stanford University Press.

Participant B

Sex _____   Age _____

Characteristics/Comments_____

Suppose that a recent personal event has put you in a depressed mood (e.g., an unexpectedly low grade on an exam, the breakup of a love relationship, or a quarrel with a close friend or relative). Check which of the following activities you are likely to engage in when you are depressed. You may check as many that apply.

_____ 1. Working on a hobby that takes concentration.

_____ 2. Writing in a diary about how you are feeling.

_____ 3. Getting away from everyone else to try to sort out your emotions.

_____ 4. Doing something with your friends.

_____ 5. Getting drunk.

_____ 6. Telling friends about how depressed you are.

_____ 7. Punching something.

_____ 8. Engaging in sports.

_____ 9. Writing a letter to someone describing your emotions.

_____ 10. Engaging in reckless behavior (e.g., driving 10 miles over the speed limit).

_____ 11. Listening to music.

_____ 12. Making a list of the reasons you are sad or depressed.

Figure from *Psychology of Women*, (3rd. ed.), by Margaret W. Matlin, copyright © 1996 by Holt, Rinehart and Winston, Inc., adapted by permission of the publisher. Based on Nolen-Hoeksema, Susan (1990). *Sex differences in depression*. Stanford, CA: Stanford University Press.

Participant C

Sex _____   Age _____

Characteristics/Comments_____

Suppose that a recent personal event has put you in a depressed mood (e.g., an unexpectedly low grade on an exam, the breakup of a love relationship, or a quarrel with a close friend or relative). Check which of the following activities you are likely to engage in when you are depressed. You may check as many that apply.

_____   1.   Working on a hobby that takes concentration.

_____   2.   Writing in a diary about how you are feeling.

_____   3.   Getting away from everyone else to try to sort out your emotions.

_____   4.   Doing something with your friends.

_____   5.   Getting drunk.

_____   6.   Telling friends about how depressed you are.

_____   7.   Punching something.

_____   8.   Engaging in sports.

_____   9.   Writing a letter to someone describing your emotions.

_____   10.   Engaging in reckless behavior (e.g., driving 10 miles over the speed limit).

_____   11.   Listening to music.

_____   12.   Making a list of the reasons you are sad or depressed.

Participant D

Sex _____   Age _____

Characteristics/Comments_____

Suppose that a recent personal event has put you in a depressed mood (e.g., an unexpectedly low grade on an exam, the breakup of a love relationship, or a quarrel with a close friend or relative). Check which of the following activities you are likely to engage in when you are depressed. You may check as many that apply.

_____ 1.   Working on a hobby that takes concentration.

_____ 2.   Writing in a diary about how you are feeling.

_____ 3.   Getting away from everyone else to try to sort out your emotions.

_____ 4.   Doing something with your friends.

_____ 5.   Getting drunk.

_____ 6.   Telling friends about how depressed you are.

_____ 7.   Punching something.

_____ 8.   Engaging in sports.

_____ 9.   Writing a letter to someone describing your emotions.

_____ 10. Engaging in reckless behavior (e.g., driving 10 miles over the speed limit).

_____ 11. Listening to music.

_____ 12. Making a list of the reasons you are sad or depressed.

Figure from *Psychology of Women*, (3rd. ed.), by Margaret W. Matlin, copyright © 1996 by Holt, Rinehart and Winston, Inc., adapted by permission of the publisher. Based on Nolen-Hoeksema, Susan (1990). *Sex differences in depression*. Stanford, CA: Stanford University Press.

PROJECT 11.5

COMMUNITY SERVICES: A FIELD VISIT

Purpose: This exercise is designed to have you conduct an in-depth evaluation of a community agency that provides services for men, women, or children with mental health disorders or who have experienced rape, assault, or other forms of abuse.

Instructions: Identify an agency in your community that provides mental health and protective services for women, men, and children. This might include counseling centers, rape crisis centers, shelters for battered partners and their children, shelters for homeless gay/lesbian/bisexual youths, etc.

Be sure to call ahead to make an appointment with the director or some other person in charge. Inform that person that you are a student in this class and that you would like to spend approximately an hour with them at their convenience so that you might learn more about the agency. If you choose to go in small groups, make sure you let your contact person know this ahead of time. An interview format is provided at the end of this exercise. Include any information packets or brochures with your exercise.

1. Review the material in your text about the target population and the problems it faces. How well would you say this agency meets the unique needs of the target population?

2.   What is your assessment of the program, including its strengths and
     weaknesses?

3.   Relate your visit to any relevant material covered in the text or in class.
     What were your feelings and impressions about your visit? What did you
     gain from it?

Field Site Interview Format

1.   Name of the institution or agency and contact person:

2.   Location, hours of operation:

3.   Description of the setting:

4.   Purpose of the agency (why was it established?):

5.   Functions of the agency (general purposes of its programs and services):

6.   Target population (what types/kinds of people do they serve?):

7.   How does the agency serve diverse populations? How does it address culturally specific issues?

8.   How many people are on staff? What are their duties?

9. Are volunteers used? If so, how?

10. What types of prevention education is offered to staff? Clients?

11. What are the challenges faced by this agency?

12. What is your (the contact person) evaluation of the strengths of the agency? Its weaknesses?

13. How can people become involved in this agency?

CHAPTER 12

SOCIAL AND PERSONAL CHANGE

PROJECT 12.1

DOING GENDER

Purpose: This exercise is designed to have you consider how you negotiate gender in your everyday interactions.

Instructions: Candace West and Don Zimmerman (1987) have argued that gender is not what someone *is* but what someone *does*. They point out that many social interactions are organized around gender. Indeed, gender could be thought of as emerging from social interaction. According to this perspective, men and women behave according to scripts, many of which evolve around cultural assumptions of the essential nature of men and women (and norms of heterosexuality). They point out that "doing gender" involves adjusting one's behavior to make it consistent with social expectations for one's sex.

1. Identify three instances from your past that are examples of doing gender. What were the circumstances? Who were you with?

2. Describe at least one instance from your past when you violated gender roles and did gender in a way that was inappropriate for your sex. What were the consequences?

3. Now that you have taken this course, how has your awareness of doing gender changed? Provide at least one example.

4. Reflecting on the material from this course, in what ways do gender roles serve as a form of social control?

5. Having taken this course, how would you like to change your process of doing gender in the future?

Reference: West, Candace, & Zimmerman, Don H. (1987). Doing gender. *Gender and Society*, *1*, 125–151.

PROJECT 12.2

A CONSCIOUSNESS-RAISING ACTIVITY

Purpose: This exercise is designed to have you discuss at least one important issue from this course with someone close to you.

Instructions: Think about a positive action toward women and/or men that is something you would not or could not have done prior to taking this course. Think about the topics covered in the course, and how the experiences of different women and men were represented. Then perform a liberating act that is positive, consciousness-raising (that is, for you and for others), and representative of the course's themes.

Your action must be nonviolent (not harming yourself or others, either mentally or physically) and must be legal. You might choose to talk with your mother or father and share an experience you had in the class, create a work of art that is affirming to men and women, construct a Web page with information about gender issues, volunteer to work as a speaker for HIV and AIDS awareness, etc. The actual action is up to you.

1. Describe the act you performed. What did you do?

2. Explain why this action served to raise your consciousness and/or that of those around you.

3. Analyze your feelings and thoughts afterward. For example, how did you feel about this issue before taking this course? In comparison, what are your feelings about this issue now? Also, how did other people around you respond?

PROJECT 12.3

RESEARCHING GENDER ACTIVISM

Purpose: This exercise is designed to increase your awareness of social groups that are engaged in gender activism.

Instructions: Research one social activist group organized around gender issues. This might include a feminist women's group, a faction of the men's movement, or a gay/lesbian/bisexual rights organization. Good sources would be newspapers, news magazines, or the Internet and World Wide Web.

1. Describe the organization you researched. Where is it located? Is it a formal or informal group? Approximately how many members does it have?

2. What is the organization's stated purpose? What are its goals?

3.   Does the organization lobby for political change? If so, how successful has it been?

4.   Does the organization take the approach that "the personal is political"? If so, how?

5.   Is diversity in race, ethnicity, class, and/or sexual orientation embraced? If so, how?

6.   How does someone become involved with this agency?

PROJECT 12.4

GETTING SEX AND GENDER INTO THE CURRICULUM

Purpose: This exercise is designed to have you consider how gender studies might be mainstreamed into the university curriculum.

Instructions: Think about one or more topics from this course that could be incorporated into a lecture in a course with which you are familiar. Consider an introductory course in psychology, sociology, anthropology, mathematics, literature, nursing, etc., that you recently have taken. For example, it might be useful to incorporate the issue of heterosexism and gender bias into the lecture on research methodology in an introductory psychology course. Or, the division of household labor and child-care tasks along gender lines could be used to supplement a lecture on work and the family in an introductory sociology course. Gender differences and similarities in cognitive abilities could be discussed in an education or mathematics course and possibly a physiology course. Be creative!

1. What is the topic and course you have selected?

2. Research this topic in the library. Identify four journal articles published within the last five to ten years that will serve as your primary references.

3. Prepare an annotated bibliography of these references to hand in with your assignment.

4. Prepare a lecture outline. Address the following issues:

    a. How does this literature fit in with the research and theory for the course?

    b. How do power relations relate to this topic? Are racism, sexism, and heterosexism considered?

    c. How is the concept of gender differences considered? Are gender differences considered along with gender similarities?

5. What new slant or angle does your lecture give to this course?

Adapted from *Exploring / Teaching the Psychology of Women* (2nd ed.) by Michele A. Paludi by permission of the State University of New York Press. © 1996 State University of New York.